Jesus – Safe, Tender, Extreme
Copyright © 2006 by Adrian Plass

Requests for information should be addressed to:
Zondervan, *Grand Rapids, Michigan 49530*

Library of Congress Cataloging-in-Publication Data

Plass, Adrian.
    Jesus – safe, tender, extreme / Adrian Plass.
       p. cm.
    ISBN-10: 0-310-25784-0
    ISBN-13: 978-0-310-25784-4
    1. Jesus Christ – Person and offices. 2. Spirituality – Anecdotes. 3. Plass,
Adrian. I. Title.
    BT203.P53 2006
    232 — dc22
                                       2005016640

Adrian Plass asserts the moral right to be identified as the author of this work.

This edition printed on acid-free paper.

Interior design by Beth Shagene

Printed in the United States of America

05 06 07 08 09 10 11 • 17 16 15 14 13 12 11 10 9 8 7 6 5 4 3 2 1

This book is dedicated to my wife's mother,
Kathleen Rosa Ormerod.
Her life was a gift to others.
All she asked in return was a few flowers
and the love of her family and friends.

CONTENTS

PART THREE: EXTREME JESUS

FOREWORD
BY JOHN ORTBERG

More than a century ago, Scottish author George Mac-Donald wrote a book called *Thomas Wingfold, Curate*. It is the story of a young pastor who–in spite of his job–suddenly finds that he doesn't know what he believes. His awareness of his doubt is God's first gift to him. His next gift is a desire to believe. His next gift is a wise spiritual guide who can help him navigate his doubts and questions and desires; and who focuses him on actually coming to seek to do what it is that Jesus asks.

At one point someone asks Wingfold if he still considers giving up the curacy. His response–which I won't take the time to quote here–moved me so deeply that the first time I heard it (being read on tape as I was driving my car) I had to pull the car over because I couldn't drive through the tears. He did not yet *believe*, Wingfold said. At least not fully, not completely. But he was convinced that if what Jesus said was not true; if there is not a God who is worthy of being the Loving Father whom Jesus described, then all of life is not worth a single tear that has been wept over it in the history of this sorry dark world. He is not yet convinced that Christianity is true in the way he wants to be convinced; but he is sure that Jesus is the only game in town.

* * *

What I love about this book by Adrian Plass is that it strikes just this same deeply honest, humanly humble, Jesus-intoxicated note. Adrian is remarkably candid about his own questions and searching—"champion of the Doubt Olympics" several times over. There is never a hint of triumphalism or hydroplaning over the difficult issues. He writes as a critical evangelical who embraces and challenges the community that has shaped him. He loves the church, and hopes for the church, and has been deeply hurt by the church, and cannot stop longing for the church.

Often when people spend decades communicating about the faith, as Adrian has, they tend to go on spiritual autopilot. They come to know what kind of stories will gain attention; what kind of questions are safe to ask, what kind of answers are expected and will gain applause.

For Adrian, though, what ends up as a dialogue with you and me begins as a musing deep within his soul; or perhaps as the kind of conversation with God that we find being held in Scripture by folks like Moses and Abraham and Jonah—questioning and complaining and thanking and fearful reverence and tender friendship and fierce determination spilling over in no particular order. It is especially a reflection about Jesus, who is safe enough to hide in, tender enough to trust, extreme enough to call us to life beyond ourselves.

* * *

Authors are generally asked to describe their target audience—who is this book for? Often in our day target audiences get pretty niched: left-handed babysitters or mechanics who like Dylan Thomas. This is a book for honest, thoughtful people who would like to know Jesus better. It is written by someone who is convinced that Jesus is the only game in town.

John Ortberg, June 2005

INTRODUCTION

Writing this book has been a strange, intense experience. In horticultural terms, my intention was to grow a tidy little shrub with a few decently spaced blooms and a general air of dignified symmetry. From the beginning it has not been like that. The roots of this project have plunged deeper into the dark earth than I had ever expected, while unmanageable fronds, tendrils, and trailing vines have shot out wildly in all directions and to all heights, searching for the light.

The light is Jesus. That much at least has been clear to me at every stage of my writing. I wanted to explore the fact that he has brought ultimate safety, tenderness, and a profound sense of adventure into my life. I believe I have done that, and as all good explorers will testify, the best possible way for an expedition to end is by coming home. We begin with Jesus, and if we have travelled by the correct route, we will certainly end with him as well.

A singular problem in the assembly of this book, if it really was a problem, arose from our immediate family circumstances. Shortly before I was due to begin writing, my wife's mother was brought home from the hospital, diagnosed with an aggressive, incurable cancer. The awareness of her presence and her suffering in our converted dining room had a

profound effect on my thoughts and emotions as I sat down
to begin work each day. Everything in me, and especially in
my faith, seemed to be excavated and exposed by the vividly
immediate presence of one who was about to finally discover
exactly what lies behind all these spiritual concepts that we
so easily wrap up in words. It made me determined to keep
heaven and earth locked together in all the things that I might
say. It made me want to tell the truth without pulling any
punches. Lots of truth. Truth about all the good, bad, wonderful, silly, dreadful, puzzling, disappointing, heartwarming
things that happen when ordinary Christians like you and me
seriously set out to follow Jesus in the real world.

This is certainly not a memoir. Testimony books, as you
know, are complete stories, usually tidied up and made as
coherent as possible for the benefit of the reader. They have
their place, but they do not meet the need of ordinary struggling Christians to understand that they can be part of the
glory of God's work in this world despite the fact that their
faith and their feelings are untidy and inconsistent and will
probably remain like that until the grave. And I certainly
had no interest in writing one of those unremittingly positive
treatises that fails to deal with life as it is actually lived. The
result is perhaps less clearly defined than I had planned – but
hopefully much more authentic. Jesus is not safe on Monday,
tender on Tuesday, and extreme on Wednesday. What would
he do for the rest of the week?

After being away from home for some weeks recently,
I had to sit myself down and reply to nearly two hundred
emails from all parts of the world. The vast majority of them
were from people who were able to keep on going, or return
to Christ, or come to Christ for the first time, or simply see a
little light at the end of the tunnel, because God had spoken
to them through accounts of personal vulnerability.

That is what I do. That seems to be my job. I am not a teacher in any orthodox sense. I am not a theologian. I am not a preacher; I cannot preach to save my life. I am simply allowed to be a man with a broom, sweeping away the rubbish that prevents others from passing further in and further up, and I tend to do this by talking about what Jesus does and doesn't do in my life.

He is safe, he is tender, and he is extreme. This book is soaked with those things.

There are a lot of stories in these pages. My experience has been that people learn more about this strange thing called "following Jesus" from stories about what actually happens than they ever will from theory. However inadequately, I try to follow the example of Jesus himself in this. The accounts of my own walk with him that I have recorded here are not just about what happens to me; they are about what happens to *us*. We get it wrong, we get it right. We learn very quickly, and we learn very slowly. We find great encouragement, and we sink to the lowest place that it is possible to be. God seems to be absent, God appears to be gloriously present. Mist clears, mist forms. We believe with all our hearts, we doubt everything. He makes us laugh, he makes us cry. Terrifyingly, he calls us to talk to people in supermarket queues; frustratingly, he tells us to keep our mouths shut in country cafés. He gives us little treats, he gets very cross. He whispers sweet words to us at the worst times. These are just a few of the things that constitute the lifeblood of living with Jesus. I would like readers to be reassured and comforted and challenged and frightened and instructed and stirred up and convicted and amused and upset by the wide-ranging, granular reality of what actually happens to Christians who try to live with their Master, as opposed to what is supposed to happen.

The longer sections of the book combine experience and reflection on those Christian issues that seem more and more crucial to me as I approach my twentieth year of speaking and writing about Jesus. In one sense I am probably wasting my time, because I am like a man walking through a maze who continually finds himself returning to the centre. Every avenue I have ever taken in my thinking and writing seems to lead back to a place where I am reminded that total commitment to Jesus is the only way to achieve true safety and real usefulness. Have I achieved this? No, I have not, but I want to, and I am trying.

At the end of each section you will find verbal snapshots of landmarks and events in my walk with Jesus. They are written in the present tense, and they are accounts of things that have really happened. They are true. Some are from the past, while others, as you will discover, are things that happened when I was in the middle of writing this book. Among these snapshots you will find everything from jubilation to despair, from peace to panic, from obedience to rebellion, from humour to tragedy. Please be with me in these moments and reflect on your own history of travelling with the Son of God. We are all in the same boat, and I know that quite violent storms do get up sometimes, but it's okay. The one with the power to calm is still with us and always will be.

I have included a selection of prayers at the end of the book. Say them with me if you think they might be helpful in your journey.

Safe, tender, and extreme. Those are the aspects of Jesus that I have always loved. I hope and pray that you will discover these qualities in him as you make your way through the tangled growth that I place before you here. God bless you, all those whom you love, and, of course, every single one of your enemies.

PART ONE

SAFE JESUS

Thoughts and Reflections
on the Safe Jesus

CHAPTER 1

SAFE IN THE LOVE OF JESUS, SAFE IN THE BODY OF CHRIST

A t this very moment, as I write, in the room at the end of the hall across from my study, someone is dying.

Kathleen Rosa Ormerod is my wife's mother and my good friend. She is eighty-eight years old and has terminal cancer. Three weeks ago, one week before Christmas, we made the decision that Kathleen should leave the hospital and spend her remaining days, weeks, or months in our house. She is confined to bed, and what a bed it is, one of those special electric ones that you feel might even perform a backward somersault if you pressed its multitudinous buttons in the correct permutation. This superbed stands in the room that until now has functioned as our dining room.

We want this to be a place for her to live in, not just the equivalent of a hospital ward. Fortunately, it is an ideal room for the purpose, bright, cosy, and enfolding, yet with a sense of being connected to the rest of the world. The windows and the glass doors are responsible for creating this effect. There are three windows, two large ones opening out towards the area at the front of the house, and another smaller one facing the backyard. In addition, there are two glass-panelled doors, the one directly in front of her giving a view of the hall and the stairs, and the other, diagonally to her right, looking through

to the kitchen, which is where everything of any real importance has always happened in our home–talking, eating, sitting around, all those crucial things. She is effectively right at
the centre of our family activity. She can see people arriving
and leaving and moving from room to room and working in
the kitchen and passing up and down the stairs. Her room is
ablaze with flowers, sent and delivered to the house by friends
and family who know how much Bridget's mum has always
loved growing things. Stoic though she is, it is a matter of
great sadness to Kathleen that it will not be possible for her
to see the flowers growing in the garden of her own house this
springtime. It breaks my heart for her. How sad it must be to
feel that you have probably seen your last springtime.

However, if you have no choice but to die and you cannot leave your bed, this is not the worst corner of the world
in which to find yourself. That is Kathleen's continually
expressed point of view, and I agree with her. She deserves this
comfort and consideration. She is a toiler of the old school, a
person who has given to others all through her life. A hard-
working, consistently obedient servant of the Lord for more
than eight decades, she has merited every good and helpful
thing that can be made available to her.

We all pay a price though. For Kathleen there is the frus-
tration in this last phase of her life of constantly having to
take from others. On the day when she first arrived at our
house after leaving the hospital, she said she wanted to ask
me something.

"Adrian," she said, "I want you to be absolutely truthful with me. Is my being here going to disrupt your family
celebrations or get in the way of your day-to day living? Be
honest with me."

"Good gracious, no," I replied. "We always like to have
someone sleeping in a hospital bed in our dining room over the
Christmas period. We'd find anything else very odd indeed."

Kathleen laughed a great deal at this, but it was also a step on the road to acceptance of the fact that the independence she values so much is not possible now. It is not her way to take without giving in return. Now she has no choice.

For my wife some things are painfully difficult to watch. Bridget sat beside her demented father as he died only months ago, and since then she has hardly had the time or space to grieve his passing. Kathleen was never a bulky person. Now she is very thin – horribly, frighteningly thin. Both of us find it very hard to look at her outstretched fleshless arm, to see the way the skin goes sliding down that brittle stick of bone like silk gliding along a polished wooden curtain pole. It is the cancer that does it. It would make no difference how much she ate. Like some ravening fungoid monster, the hungry killer inside takes a huge part of all the goodness and nutrition that goes into her body, feeding itself and growing larger and more blindly, grossly dominant by the day. We find it strange to look at her, so slight, so fragile, and so inoffensive, and to know that this ugly thing is murdering her by inches.

At the end of the day, assisted by medication, she sleeps like a dead person, skin china white, her mouth hanging open on her chest, her head tilted to one side. Recently, exchanging notes, my wife and I discovered that after she has settled for the night, we are both in the habit of peering fearfully in through the glass panels of the door that connects her room to the hall, studying her with round-eyed, fearful concentration, hoping to detect in the rise and fall of the emaciated chest beneath her nightdress that she is still with us. Hard though it is to admit, there are times, especially when she has had a depressingly difficult, uncomfortable day, when we half hope that her shallow breathing will stop. We wonder if God might allow her to slip quietly away to join her beloved George, in a place where, for him, there is no more panic-stricken confusion and, for her, no more commodes and catheters and bedsores and all the other varieties of personal humiliation that polite and private people so dislike.

At night we take Kathleen's breathing to bed with us. Bridget has bought one of those baby monitors so that her mother can call her in the night if she needs help urgently. The transmitter is downstairs beside Kathleen, and the receiver is in our bedroom. I found this very strange at first, and I shall never become accustomed to it. It is as though another person's soul is trapped in the little white plastic contraption with the glowing red light that stands on a shelf in the corner of our bedroom. Every night now, after I have switched off my bedside lamp, there are, unnervingly, two sets of human sounds in the blackness apart from my own, and the overlapping rhythms of two clocks ticking, one of them on our wall, and the other standing on the little table next to Kathleen as she sleeps. The ticking of her little square clock continues like the beating of a healthy heart, but there are moments when the sound of Kathleen's breathing seems to be arrested altogether. When this happens Bridget will sometimes sit bolt upright in bed, straining her ears to detect the slightest evidence of a breath being taken. More than once she has begged me to go downstairs and look through the glass door to check that her mother is still alive. Nights are far from easy at present. Love and death and fear excavate the soul, producing strange, convoluted dreams and hours of uneasy consciousness.

As members of the family from more distant parts have made the trip to visit Kathleen, I have seen a deep sadness in her after their departure. She explains that on each occasion she is conscious that this may be the last time she sees her visitor in this world. Sometimes she has a little cry, especially over her diminishing powers, a general feeling of having nothing useful or practical to contribute to the world around her. Of course, we reassure her, but she is not silly. She would say all the same things to us if we were in her position.

These things are deeply upsetting. Bridget cries a lot. I am not made like that, in the sense that I tend to do most of my crying in private, but I am full of feeling. We need each other very much at the moment. Two things help us as a couple above all others. One is the fact that we have been good friends, thank God, since we married thirty-three years ago. The other is that we have always wanted to have Jesus at the centre of our day-to-day living. I think he has been there most of the time, although honesty compels me to admit that he might have been displaced at certain points in our lives. Who am I kidding? I know full well he has. But never mind. At the very least God is as forgiving as my own mother was, and she was a person who handed out that precious commodity as though she had been put in charge of an inexhaustible store.

Now we are glad that both of the things I have mentioned are true. These are difficult days. We need to look after each other. We are not doing too badly. A couple of times, when the tension has become unbearable, we have found ourselves having foolish, meaningless little arguments, sniping at each other about nothing at all. They don't last long. We are like children. God is our Father. We shall be all right.

So there we are. Or rather, here I am, sitting at my computer trying to write a book about following Jesus while someone is dying in the room at the other end of the hall. The presence of Bridget's mother, and the imminence of her departure to the place where we hope that all questions will be answered and all problems solved, has what I can only call a profoundly "editing" effect on the things that I am thinking and writing.

* * *

Jesus said to her, "I am the resurrection and the life. He who believes in me will live, even though he dies; and whoever lives and believes in me will never die. Do you believe this?"

"Yes, Lord," she told him, "I believe that you are the Christ, the Son of God, who was to come into the world."

These stirring words from the eleventh chapter of John's gospel had better be true, hadn't they? For Kathleen's sake, I mean. When you know for sure that your days on this earth are numbered, there has to be a positive prospect of some kind to lift and draw you over the inevitable final obstacle of dying. The other day I asked her about this.

"Are you very worried about dying?"

She answered without any visible hesitation.

"Oh no, I'm not at all worried about being dead. I know what I believe. I'm very comfortable and well looked after, and I'm not in any pain at the moment." She paused for a second or two, and then continued in a much softer voice, "I don't like the idea of leaving you all behind though."

I hope that when my time comes I shall be as sure in my beliefs as Kathleen seems to be. She is quite safe in her faith. No wonder Jesus said that we must become like little children. Some things are much easier to believe effortlessly when you are small. For example, when my mother's mother died, I was devastated. I missed her horribly, but when my mummy told me that Nana was in heaven and that I would see her again one day, I was comforted on the deepest level and trusted implicitly that this would be so. Do I still have that implicit trust in the same innocently optimistic way? No. Yes. Sometimes. Absolutely without question. Not in the slightest. Only on Thursdays.

I am working towards being the child Jesus wants me to be, and he is helping. I lift my arms towards my Father in heaven and ask him to put his arms round what I am, not what I ought to be. What else can I do?

A SACRED MYSTERY

As I have said, this book is supposed to be about Jesus, and I have been asking myself where he is in all the things that are happening to my mother-in-law, and what the situation might teach us about him. A couple of these answers interest and encourage me.

One is connected to the way in which Christians handle the idea of death and departure from the people they love. Despite her firm belief in a life with God after death, Kathleen hates the prospect of leaving all of us behind and would certainly not choose to die if she was given the option of recovering her health and enjoying a few more years in the land of the living. Is there not abundant evidence in the gospels to suggest that Jesus was the same? Poor Jesus. True man and true God. Filled with pain because of that very fact on more than one occasion.

As Jesus was approaching the end of his earthly ministry, we know that he wept and was very troubled. Hardly surprising, is it? The shadow of the imminent dislocation of earth and heaven was darkening his heart. He was weeping because all the loves were tearing him apart and were about to spread him piecemeal across the universe. Look at this passage from the gospel of John.

> "Very truly, I tell you, unless a grain of wheat falls into the earth and dies, it remains just a single grain; but if it dies, it bears much fruit. Those who love their life lose it, and those who hate their life in this world will keep it for eternal life. Whoever serves me must follow me, and where I am, there will my servant be also. Whoever serves me, the Father will honour.
>
> "Now my soul is troubled. And what should I say– 'Father, save me from this hour'? No, it is for this reason that I have come to this hour. Father, glorify your name." (12:24–28 NRSV)

Here, in these two paragraphs, we are allowed to witness divinity and humanity in the mind of Jesus, the one following hard on the heels of the other. The statement and the struggle, the preaching and the pain, the toil and the trouble. The theory is right, the theology is unimpeachable, the intention is pure, but still the wholly human heart of Jesus cries out like a child against the immensity of the thing he is about to undertake. I sometimes replay those words in my mind as you or I might say them.

"It's just too much! I can't stand it. Oh Father, I could ask you to rescue me. I could beg you just to take this terrible, ghastly prospect away from me, and you would do it because you love me, but what would be the point of that? It's the very thing I came for. It's the reason I'm alive. It's for you. Okay, I'm all right now. Glorify your name."

And here is Matthew's account of Jesus in the garden of Gethsemane. Try to pretend you have never read it. You won't be able to, but do your best.

> Then Jesus went with them to a place called Gethsemane; and he said to his disciples, "Sit here while I go over there and pray." He took with him Peter and the two sons of Zebedee, and began to be grieved and agitated. Then he said to them, "I am deeply grieved, even to death; remain here, and stay awake with me." And going a little farther, he threw himself on the ground and prayed, "My Father, if it is possible, let this cup pass from me; yet not what I want but what you want." Then he came to the disciples and found them sleeping; and he said to Peter, "So, could you not stay awake with me one hour? Stay awake and pray that you may not come into the time of trial; the spirit indeed is willing, but the flesh is weak." Again he went away for the second time and prayed, "My Father, if this cannot pass unless I drink it, your will be done." Again he came and found them sleeping, for their eyes were heavy. So leaving them again, he went away and prayed for the third

time, saying the same words. Then he came to the disciples and
said to them, "Are you still sleeping and taking your rest? See,
the hour is at hand, and the Son of Man is betrayed into the
hands of sinners. Get up, let us be going. See, my betrayer is at
hand." (26:36–46 NRSV)

Luke adds, in verses that some ancient manuscripts leave out,
that when Jesus prayed in the garden, his sweat became like
"great drops of blood falling down on the ground" (22:44
NRSV).

A gargantuan struggle.

Here is a question, then. When Jesus said that the spirit
was willing but the flesh was weak, whom do you think he
was talking about? I spend my life catching up with things
that other people already know, so it has only just occurred
to me that Jesus is talking about himself as much or more
than he is talking about the poor old, heavy-eyed disciples,
who couldn't have had the faintest idea what was going on,
or what was about to happen. Jesus was without sin, not
without temptation. He really did not want to go through
with the next stage of the task, did he? Who can blame him?

As with Bridget's mother, the prospect of leaving behind
the people he loved was unspeakably sad for Jesus, but of
course it was vastly more than that. There is a sacred mystery at the heart of the suffering that Jesus was about to go
through. The cross was an appalling instrument of torture,
but others, before and since, have suffered as much and con-
siderably more in a physical sense. No, there was an element
or species of pain in the crucifixion of Jesus that I am incapable of even beginning to comprehend. We know that he went
through the agony of being forsaken by his Father, and that
may have been the darkest, most bitter moment of them all.
Is it possible that in that supremely awful instant, his worst
nightmare of all appeared to be coming true?

Perhaps, regardless of everything that had happened, he was not the Messiah. Perhaps his divinity was a complex illusion. Perhaps he was just a man hanging on a piece of wood. Perhaps it was all a ghastly mistake. He could have stayed and compromised and got married and had children and grown old and enjoyed many, many springtimes.

I have no idea if that is true or not. It is a matter of interpretation and conjecture, but we are allowed to employ conjecture. Writer and broadcaster Rabbi Lionel Blue once made the point that Judaism was his home, not his prison. It seems to me that this is a good perspective for Christians as well. In the spiritual sense there is no such thing as those dreadful conditions of agoraphobia or claustrophobia in the kingdom of God. The safer and happier we are in our home, the more comfortable we shall be in popping out to explore what's going on down the road.

Whatever we do not know for sure, we can be fairly certain that although he had known the joys of heaven "before Abraham was", Jesus was terrified of what was to come, but he also knew that true security was only to be found through obedience. As always, he said yes to his Father. There is a tantalising paradox at the heart of all this that has always been just beyond the grasp of definition, certainly as far as I am concerned. It is a cloud or mist formed from a multitude of apparent contradictions.

Man and God. Obey or disobey. Filled with the Spirit and forsaken. Dead and alive. Failed and triumphant. Natural and supernatural. Ordinary and extraordinary. Law and grace. Of this world and not of this world.

Sometimes I am almost giddy with a vertiginous sense that I am right on the edge of a revelation so filled with light and love and final reassurance that nothing will ever be able to hurt me or disturb my peace again, and lunatic though it sounds, I sense in my heart of hearts that what is revealed will undoubtedly and mysteriously be something that I already know. Perhaps that sounds as though it means nothing, but I recall C. S. Lewis's description of how when we hear or see true beauty, there is an aching sensation of homesickness for something or somebody that we have never had and never will have. The instinct for heaven. It is there within us. We live with it, and it is our constant companion. It does, however, wear many strange and almost impenetrable disguises.

The same Jesus who sweated blood at Gethsemane is in this house with Kathleen and with us. She is perfectly safe. He will take her hand when the time comes for her to go, and I do pray that the going will not be hard.

TOUCHING JESUS

As Kathleen dies, Jesus is also with us in the form of our church. People sometimes tell me off for attacking the church, but I have never wanted or set out to do that. I love the Body of Christ, the church, that is, and over the last few weeks, Bridget and Kathleen and I have seen what that three-word phrase can mean when the hard times come. Yes, I know that love and care can be just as evident in secular communities, but that's okay. God invented love. The world he made might be fallen, but you can see his fingerprints and the marks of his feet all over creation, sometimes in the most unexpected places.

We have felt very loved. Do you remember what Paul said about the Body of Christ?

> If all were a single member, where would the body be? As it is, there are many members, yet one body. The eye cannot say to the hand, "I have no need of you," nor again the head to the feet, "I have no need of you." On the contrary, the members of the body that seem to be weaker are indispensable, and

those members of the body that we think less honourable we clothe with greater honour, and our less respectable members are treated with greater respect; whereas our more respectable members do not need this. But God has so arranged the body, giving the greater honour to the inferior member, that there may be no dissension within the body, but the members may have the same care for one another. If one member suffers, all suffer together with it; if one member is honoured, all rejoice together with it. (1 Corinthians 12:19–26 NRSV)

The part of the body that we belong to has certainly suffered together with Kathleen and with us. Quite apart from support in prayer, help has come in many forms. We have a young, explosively energetic border terrier named Lucy, who on a number of occasions has been whisked away for the walks that she so adores. People have cooked for us and sat in for us so that we can have a break. They have visited and sent flowers and cards. Our converted dining room is beginning to acquire the scent and the appearance of a florist's shop. The curate in charge of our church has twice brought Communion to Kathleen. She loves this and so do we. Bridget and I and Kathleen form three quarters of the congregation. It feels like an enormous treat to have the mystery and cosmic significance of the bread and wine here in this little room, just for the three of us. God has some very good ideas, do you not think? This is one of the best. Rooting the vastness of spirituality and salvation in such potent, earthy symbols as bread and wine is nothing short of a masterpiece.

Yes, the Body of Christ has sustained and lifted and protected us. It is easy to forget that these encounters with Jesus through the hands and hearts of our brothers and sisters are spiritual experiences on a par with any of the more detached and otherworldly numinous encounters that go on in formally religious situations. Why do we find this so hard to accept? Anyone who has had a family should be able to understand the principle. Bridget and I have three sons and a daughter, and very few things give us more pleasure than knowing that they are getting together, looking after each other, and enjoying being in one another's company. When those things are happening, it is like a vindication or validation of our parenthood. Yes, all right, in our case there may well be a rather childish element in that response, but it does help us to understand how our heavenly Father feels about the members of his family loving and caring for each other. Here is Jesus on the same subject towards the end of John's gospel.

> "This is my commandment, that you love one another as I have loved you. No one has greater love than this, to lay down one's life for one's friends. You are my friends if you do what I command you. I do not call you servants any longer, because the servant does not know what the master is doing; but I have called you friends, because I have made known to you everything that I have heard from my Father. You did not choose me but I chose you. And I appointed you to go and bear fruit, fruit that will last, so that the Father will give you whatever you ask him in my name. I am giving you these commands so that you may love one another." (15:12–17 NRSV)

With all due respect, there is just a hint of the worried mother about this, is there not?

"I have to go away, so you must promise to look after each other. You won't forget, will you? Love one another. It's so important to me. Promise you will."

The sacred and mystical truth is that when we Christians touch each other, we are touching Jesus. When that touch is the touch of care and love, heaven smiles on us, and the same God who speaks through the twenty-seventh verse of the first chapter of the book of James says, with the satisfaction of a proud parent, "Just look at that! Now that is what I call true religion."

I thank God for Kathleen Rosa Ormerod, for her stubbornness and her generosity and her loyalty and her practical care and her unfailing love for her friends and her principled way of living and her faith and her courage and for the vulnerability that we have been privileged to see in these last weeks. I thank God for all that she is and all that she has done. I would like her to live, but above all I want God's best for her, whatever that might be.

CHAPTER 2

FREEDOM, SAFETY, AND THE VALUE OF TRUTH

I shall attempt the challenging task of telling some truth in this and the next chapter, not, I hasten to add, to create a contrast with all the other parts of the book, but in the context of specific areas where we in the church have become very adept at kidding ourselves. Of course, my truth may not be the same as yours, but after twenty years of talking to Christians all over the world, I shall be more than a little surprised if the gap is a consistently wide one.

Before we get into specific issues, though, what has the truth to do with safety, and why does it matter so much? Put at its simplest, if we really want to be secure in the most profound sense, we have no choice but to dwell in the truth, however challenging that may be. If we are defending ourselves or our faith or the way that we live or the life of the church in any other terms but truthful ones, then we have parted company with the Spirit of truth. In those circumstances we are on our own and dangerously exposed.

The most significant changes in my life began with a desire to discard the piles of nonsense that were cluttering up my own Christian life and to find spiritual safety by seeing the truth about myself and my faith with as much clarity as it was possible for God to grant my clouded vision. Since the very earliest days of the writing and speaking phase of my life, there is one verse that has underpinned and inspired my efforts more than any other. It is something that Jesus said, and it occurs in the eighth chapter of the gospel of John. I am sure you will recognise it immediately.

> To the Jews who had believed him, Jesus said, "If you hold to my teaching, you are really my disciples. Then you will know the truth, and the truth will set you free." (8:31–32)

The final six words of this passage have always meant a great deal to me, but as anyone who has ever set out to tell the complete truth will know, it is by no means always comfortable. Sometimes it hurts. Sometimes it makes me laugh. Sometimes it makes me feel very silly indeed. Sometimes it makes me weep. Sometimes it becomes clear that, as with Adam and Eve, the naked truth is not what is required. There are times when it is embarrassing and needs to be decently covered.

THE TRUTH ABOUT US;
THE TRUTH ABOUT GOD

Here is one thing that is becoming clear to me. There are two essential areas of truth that we need to deal with if we are interested in encouraging others to come home to the Father. One is the truth about us, about you and me as we really are, and the other is the untainted truth about God. If, in our efforts to pass on the good news, we try to communicate either one of these while ignoring the other, we are probably, at best, wasting our time and, at worst, creating a potentially very destructive form of confusion.

Most of us, whether we like it or not, are works in progress. God certainly knows that. We know it, if we're honest. What point is there in trying to persuade others or ourselves that this is not the case? Folk will always see through religious or moral posing in the end. People have quite often seen through some nonsense of mine. I wonder how many of God's lost and beloved children have turned disappointedly away from the idea of following Jesus because of the hypocrisy they detected in Christians, people who managed to impress them greatly on a personal level in the initial stages of their relationship and subsequently simply couldn't keep it up.

Sometimes this contrast between what we are and what we believe is graphically revealed. There is an exercise that my wife, Bridget, and I have found helpful to use with groups of thirty or forty people. Try it yourself. The results can be interesting. The aim of this exercise is twofold. The immediate aim is to write a group poem. This is usually very enjoyable and interesting, but the more important function of the activity is to show all those present that the truth about the Body of Christ is far more granular, more diverse, and, dare I say, more useful than we might have expected. This is how we do it.

First of all, it is as well to bear in mind that a lot of people freeze when they think some coyly grinning Christian sadist is about to force them into writing poetry, with the subtle implication that hell awaits those who fail to cooperate. We always make it clear that no one is actually going to write any poetry but that a collection of short, truthful, anonymous statements will, by its very nature, acquire a poetic ring when it is read aloud by one person. We give out small slips of paper to each member of the group and announce that the first poem will be entitled "Our God Is Many Things".

"Please write on your piece of paper," Bridget or I will then say, "what God is to you at this precise moment on this particular day. Don't try to be consciously poetic. Don't worry about putting down the right answer. There is no right answer other than your own private truth. Try not to write down your second, third, or fourth thoughts. Try to catch the first one before it gets disapproved of and edited, or it just flies away. Don't sign your paper. It really doesn't matter what you say, negative or positive, because no one except God will know who has written which line when we read the whole thing out. Please write clearly and briefly in capital letters, and then fold your papers and give them to one of us when we come round to collect them in a couple of minutes."

Some people are a little uneasy about all this, but the assurance of genuine anonymity is usually helpful. We end up with a little pile of thirty or forty statements, and Bridget is very skilled at reading these out on the spot, avoiding word-for-word repetition, and adding in the title and theme of the "poem" as she proceeds. The results, assembled in something very close to the random order in which they have been collected, are quite riveting and can sometimes be very moving. Here is what one group produced.

Our God is many things
He is a good Father, loving and ever-present
He is my rock
He is never with me when I need him most
A distant God, looking for reasons to punish
My best friend
The light that makes my darkness bearable

Our God is many things
The sun in winter, promising that spring will come
He has gone on holiday somewhere
The Father I never had
He is impossible to know
The essence of love
He is a mystery that death will solve

Our God is many things
He is like the sea, deep and serene
Filled with forgiveness

He loves everyone – except me
He lives in us
He must see my agony, but he doesn't do anything about it
His love keeps the world turning

Our God is many things
Awesome and mighty
The Rose of Sharon
Our God is the one who painted the rainbow
He is cold and silent, full of promises that he never seems
*   to keep*
Our God is the God of the Jews
He hears and sees all that we do

Our God is many things
The one I have been searching for all my life
A masked stranger
He helps the sky to kiss the sea
Glorious beyond words
The Father of our Lord Jesus
Nothing to write home about
Our God is many things
All I will ever want or need
I don't know what will happen to me if things don't change
*   soon*
Our God is the same yesterday, today, and tomorrow
God is love
I talk to him a lot, but does he listen?
Our God is many things

Not exactly a candidate for inclusion in your favourite hymnbook, is it? The groups that produce this kind of response are often quite startled by the things that are exposed when a small section of the Body of Christ is allowed to express inner feelings without an immediate threat from one of those clodhopping terrible twins, Condemnation and Ministry. This example of a cry from the heart of the body contains just about everything, doesn't it? There is joy and sadness and doubt and indifference and fear and pain and praise and love and deep appreciation and the kind of questioning that is all too often concealed on the dark side of the heart.

On the many occasions when we have done this exercise with groups, we have never once seen a result that presented the group as being uniformly positive and at peace. This is the way it is within the Body of Jesus on earth, and I have an idea it would be good for us to face it. We cannot avoid the issue by saying that some of the more negative comments in a poem like this must come from people who are not really Christians. That is not the case. I know it is not. So do you. Most of us go through many different phases in the course of our Christian lives. These phases range in their nature, if you are anything like me, from despair to ecstasy, but wherever we happen to be at any one time, unless something exceptionally drastic and awful has happened, we remain members of the Body.

The challenge facing every single one of us is simple but sometimes alarming. Leaving aside deliberate, persistent disobedience and sin, will we own the things, good and bad, that are happening in our brothers and sisters, as though they are happening in us, and really are part of us? If you like, it is the other side of the coin presented to us by Jesus when he spoke about the danger and undesirability of judging others in the seventh chapter of Matthew's gospel.

> "Do not judge, or you too will be judged. For in the same way you judge others, you will be judged, and with the measure you use, it will be measured to you.
>
> "Why do you look at the speck of sawdust in your brother's eye and pay no attention to the plank in your own eye? How can you say to your brother, 'Let me take the speck out of your eye,' when all the time there is a plank in your own eye? You hypocrite, first take the plank out of your own eye, and then you will see clearly to remove the speck from your brother's eye." (7:1–5)

Paul makes a very similar point in the fourteenth chapter of Romans.

> Why do you pass judgement on your brother and sister? Or you, why do you despise your brother or sister? For we will all stand before the judgement seat of God. For it is written,
> "As I live, says the Lord, every knee shall bow
> to me, and every tongue shall give praise to God."
> So then, each of us will be accountable to God.
> Let us therefore no longer pass judgement on one another, but resolve instead never to put a stumbling block or hindrance in the way of another. (14:10–13 NRSV)

Tough as it may be, and however much of a challenge to our feelings of safety and security, it is very important to God that we stand firm beside our fellow believers, whatever they may be going through. Should we not be taking turns to be Jesus for each other, and allowing the truth to be told without reacting with rejection or aggression, or by fainting decoratively like one of our modern thespian soccer players, or in the manner of some Victorian heroine who has just learned that not all men are perfect? Jesus is among us in the real world, and it is his command that we should tell the truth about ourselves and about him. That is certainly what Paul did, speaking freely about his life before conversion in the first chapter of his first letter to Timothy.

> I thank Christ Jesus our Lord, who has given me strength, that he considered me faithful, appointing me to his service. Even though I was once a blasphemer and a persecutor and a violent man, I was shown mercy because I acted in ignorance and unbelief. The grace of our Lord was poured out on me abundantly, along with the faith and love that are in Christ Jesus.
>
> Here is a trustworthy saying that deserves full acceptance: Christ Jesus came into the world to save sinners—of whom I

am the worst. But for that very reason I was shown mercy so that in me, the worst of sinners, Christ Jesus might display his unlimited patience as an example for those who would believe on him and receive eternal life. Now to the King eternal, immortal, invisible, the only God, be honor and glory for ever and ever. Amen. (1:12–17)

Additionally, in the following extract from the second book of Corinthians, Paul makes it clear that he still suffers from weaknesses, although, very frustratingly, in this life we shall never know for certain what his famous "thorn in the flesh" actually was.

> Therefore, to keep me from being too elated, a thorn was given me in the flesh, a messenger of Satan to torment me, to keep me from being too elated. Three times I appealed to the Lord about this, that it would leave me, but he said to me, "My grace is sufficient for you, for power is made perfect in weakness." So, I will boast all the more gladly of my weaknesses, so that the power of Christ may dwell in me. (12:7–9 NRSV)

The truth will set us free—I'm afraid. Where shall I start? What shall I tell the truth about? The list of candidates is a very long one, but there are four areas that immediately suggest themselves to me, two of which we shall explore in this chapter, and two in the next. Let us begin with a really juicy one.

DOUBT

Forgive me if I sound conceited, but I have won the gold medal in three consecutive Doubt Olympics and achieved silver and gold in another four. I am versatile. I never did bother to specialise. Sprint or marathon, it makes no difference. I excel in most events.

Doubt has been an adjunct to my Christian life since forty years ago, when I first told Jesus that I wanted to hear him say yes to me, just as he said it to the thief on the cross at Calvary. There have been times, notably when there has been a period of grinding, dismal ordinariness about everything I do and hear and see, when I have shrugged my shoulders and said to myself, "Why on earth do I go on believing this nonsense? We're born, we live, we die, and that's the end. Nothing else. No heaven, no hell, no nothing. Don't be silly. Stop dreaming and get on with filling up the years of life that you have left with something you'll enjoy."

When I was an even younger Christian than I am now, I used to read passages like the one that follows from the book of James and find myself trembling with apprehension.

> If any of you lacks wisdom, he should ask God, who gives generously to all without finding fault, and it will be given to him. But when he asks, he must believe and not doubt, because he who doubts is like a wave of the sea, blown and tossed by the wind. That man should not think he will receive anything from the Lord; he is a double-minded man, unstable in all he does. (1:5–8)

I got quite depressed about this. It was an inescapable fact that I frequently doubted God's ability or willingness to answer my prayers. So there it was. That was me. Hopeless. I was like a wave of the sea, a man who shouldn't have thought that he would receive anything from the Lord, a double-minded man, unstable in all he did. What hope was there for me?

To make things worse, I also read about Peter stepping out of the boat onto the water, then sinking at the second step because his faith took a sudden dip. Sudden dip? I knew for sure that I would never be able to take even that first step without the benefit of a yellow inflatable life jacket from under my seat in the boat, and a light that would come on when it came in contact with the water, and a whistle that I could blow to attract attention.

I thought about the disciples getting terrified on that other occasion in the boat with Jesus when the storm came up and he was fast asleep. If I had been there, would I have lounged serenely in the bottom of the boat, saying something faithful and optimistic like the following:

"Well, to be absolutely honest, I don't know what all the fuss is about. I wasn't troubled at all, and frankly, I'm surprised and shocked at you other chaps making such a silly commotion when you know the Lord's here and everything's perfectly in hand. Learn from the bread and fish, why don't you? I have. The poor fellow's tired out. You should have let him sleep; you really should."

No, I'm afraid not. In fact, I knew I would have been one of the first ones to tug wildly on his sleeve and go screaming around the boat begging him to wake up and *do* something.

You may or may not be surprised to hear that there have been moments at the ends of meetings, meetings in which I have been speaking passionately about the ever-present, living God, when my faith has utterly deserted me, and I am left feeling like an empty thing, a shell, hearing nothing but the faint echoes of my own prating voice in the dull inner silence that has so suddenly and unexpectedly descended. These moments are cold and dark and bewildering. I hope that you have never known them. I hope you never will. They are the pits, and they come from the pit.

There we are then. That is what I have known of doubt, or as much of it as I think it is necessary to tell you about, and on the face of it, I suppose there might seem to be a strong case for drumming me out of the Christian church. I'm supposed to be a believer, for goodness' sake, not someone who lurches along from one fragile patch of faith to another, clinging by his fingertips to the reality of Jesus. The truth is, though, that most if not all of us have travelled through the dark valley of doubt. What we need is a little honesty and encouragement. So what are the useful things that we can say about this whole area?

TRUE ABANDONMENT

I should say first of all that I have never been able to take my own advice concerning the need to give up that silly dream I mentioned just now, the one about God and following Jesus and all that nonsense, so that I can fill the rest of my life up with things I'll enjoy. I know that it would fail to answer my deepest needs. I have mentioned elsewhere that the very idea of oblivion, of hitting a dumb, dark wall at the end of life's complex, emotion-filled journey, creates an overwhelming sense of claustrophobia in me. I would rather believe and be wrong than live in a godless world. It is one of the fundamental reasons why periods of doubt usually end with my throwing myself back into the arms of God like a child who has shocked himself with a game that has become too frighteningly real to handle.

This may not sound a terribly rational thing to do, but I can tell you that it feels good, it puts me back on track, and there can be few things more theologically sound than the concept of abandoning yourself to God.

TRUE MERCY

Second, there is an injunction in the letter of Jude (probably the brother of Jesus) that we might reasonably assume to reflect the heart of God in these matters: "Be merciful to those who doubt ..." And, as Jesus himself commands in the sixth chapter of Luke's gospel: "Be merciful, just as your Father is merciful."

Yes, what a good idea. Be merciful to others when you are floating along on a cloud, feeling like Billy Graham cubed, and they are trudging their way miserably over the grey surface of the earth, wondering why they ever believed in God in the first place. It will be your turn to need encouragement next week or month or year. Be merciful towards God, who is continually hurt by the harshness with which his children sometimes judge themselves and others. Go on, be merciful.

Be merciful to yourself when doubt creeps in, and you don't want it to, but it does anyway. You know, there is a sense in which it is better to accept these negative feelings than to fight them. In recent years I have developed an approach to this problem that has been very effective for me. Try it yourself. See if it helps. This is how it goes:

When doubt knocks at the door, let him in. Sit him down in a corner, but don't entertain him, and whatever you do, don't feed him. Let him stay as long as he likes. Eventually, bored and hungry, he will let himself out, probably when your back is turned and you are busy doing something else. At best, you will forget that he was ever there; at worst, you will breathe a sigh of relief when you realise that you have regained the extra space that he has been taking up.

Now, I know that these are just words, but they are based on something much more substantial and important. Doubt doesn't actually live in your house, even if it insists on visiting from time to time. Once we have become followers of Jesus, faith is placed by God into the centre of who we are. Do you remember these verses from the second chapter of Ephesians?

> For it is by grace you have been saved, through faith – and this not from yourselves, it is the gift of God – not by works, so that no one can boast. For we are God's workmanship, created in Christ Jesus to do good works, which God prepared in advance for us to do. (2:8 – 10)

Very clear, isn't it? Faith is a gift from God, not a whim of our own, and therefore we may justly assume that just as God defaults to compassion, so we default to faith. In other words, doubt may be the dark kite that we sometimes find ourselves flying in the night, but faith is what supports our feet even when our eyes are turned elsewhere and we have forgotten the nature of the solid ground that upholds us. If God has given me the gift of faith and had it fitted by qualified angelic surgeons, it makes as much sense to tell myself that one of my legs is missing as to assume that my faith really has disappeared.

Yes, we know that faith can be lost. The Bible makes it clear that believers can be drawn away from the truth and that we can be robbed of our faith, but in the blessedly ordinary, workaday world of Christians like you and me, I think we are allowed to be quietly confident that doubt is the illusion (and what a nuisance it is) but faith is the reality.

And when I think about this, it makes so much sense on the level of my day-to-day experience as a Christian. Do you know, in the very midst of those dark and heavy experiences of doubt, I have often found myself discussing these feelings with Jesus, almost as if the issues of faith and doubt have little to do with each other. Well, in truth, I don't think they do. Such a conversation may sound somewhat neurotic, but I suspect that it is actually very sane. As the years go by, I continue to suffer from doubts, but I am agnostic to the point of atheism about their reality.

TRUE INDIVIDUALITY

My third point is about individual differences, and this is, of course, an area with much broader implications than those associated merely with doubt. We are all, to an extent, trapped within the thicket of the things we have become, and even though God redeems us, the complete breaking down of that thicket is a task that will occupy the Holy Spirit (with co-operation from us) for our entire lives. *Please* let us not be silly about this. I know there are people who cannot stand the idea that Christian living can be ragged and awkward and sometimes slow. They want glorious transfiguration or nothing. That is why, when such people are allowed to lead churches, the majority of their members are deluded, very good at pretending, or puzzled and worried about their lack of progress in comparison with the "triumphant" others. The truth, dramatically illustrated by "Our God Is Many Things", is that we Christians are not only very different people but also at widely varying stages in our understanding of what walking with Jesus really means.

For instance, Bridget and I had one friend, now gone to be with Jesus, who was such a psychological wreck after a disastrous childhood that the main function of our relationship, as far as we were concerned, was simply to assist in making the barest emotional and sometimes physical survival possible for him. Perhaps there was something else we could have done. I doubt it. I believe our task was to be Jesus for this broken life until his painful time on earth was ended and he could be perfectly healed by one breath of the healing air of heaven and by a single touch of the Father's hand. We pray and we work and we leave the miracles to God.

Given what we are, what can we do? That is the reasonable question to ask. Because God is God, we know that sometimes there will be a miraculous answer to that question, but in the majority of cases, and until that happens, we must work with what we have and what we are. That applies to doubt as much as to anything else. I offer you the following example of this principle.

I have a friend who has been a Christian for fifty years or more, since he was a teenager, in fact. Almost from the moment of his conversion, he has had a preacher's heart. What do I mean by that? I mean that he is inwardly driven to preach the good news about Jesus to anyone who will listen, as an evangelist for many years and latterly as an elder in one of our local churches. There must be people all over the United Kingdom who can trace the path of their faith back to an afternoon or evening when the words of my friend and the power of the Holy Spirit drew them to Jesus. Additionally, in terms of one-to-one contact, this man has a compassion and an absorbency that have softened countless stubborn spirits and brought relief to many, many fearful hearts. My friend is far from perfect, but he has given a lifetime of service to God, and that original teenage motivation has rarely faltered.

And yet.

This same man said to me, just the other day, "I've been trying to prepare a talk for Easter Sunday. I sat down at my desk yesterday, and I said to God, 'Look, if you exist, help me to put something useful together.' "

He was not being flippant. He meant exactly what he said. That is how my friend is made. If I had more time, I could explain to you how various negative elements of his childhood have made it very difficult for him to relax into confident sonship. Others I know have been healed in areas such as these. This man has not. It is in the doing of his work for God that the gift of faith rises in him and inhabits the words that have a capacity for changing lives. In between these occasions on which he defaults to faith and reaches out with the gospel, he is capable of sinking into a slough of despond where there is no God and where, even if there was, this stern deity would never open the gates of heaven to such an unworthy and vacillating excuse for a servant.

You may feel that my friend should have sorted all this out by now. I suppose you would have a point. I have been asking God to help him do that for many years, and if you think that your prayers will help, please go ahead and pray, but out of the corner of my eye, I note an enigmatic expression on the face of Jesus when it comes to the mention of this man.

The Lord knows my friend, and he knows me. My friend lacks assurance. I can be dreadfully inconsistent in other ways. Between us we make up a Christian who believes in the fatherhood of God and is unstintingly consistent in his dealings with others. We are the Body of Christ. Is there a better thing to be part of when you know that you fall short in many areas and cannot cope on your own? I doubt it.

HEALING

Let's move on to the second area in which we will try to shed some light and tell some truth. As far as I can see, not many people are healed by God. I hear a lot of talk about healing as I travel around the country and the world, and I read a great deal about something called holistic healing, which, as far as I can see, means that nobody gets healed but a lot of very serious nodding happens. I visited a Christian healing centre a few years ago and asked if anyone had actually been healed there. The person I was speaking to smiled enigmatically and replied, "Well, it depends what you mean by healing."

"Oh, right," I said, a little taken aback. "I suppose I mean one minute someone is sick or injured, and the next minute, or not very long afterwards, they're not. Like when Jesus was here. Lepers and blind men. That sort of thing."

"What you need to understand," explained the man, "is that we like to feel here we're setting out to heal the whole person, body, spirit, and mind."

"I see; so would that include the whole person's elbow if it wasn't working properly?"

He thought for a moment, then shook his head.

"I don't think we've had any actual physical healings of that sort, but there was a lady whose recuperation period was significantly shortened ..."

Investigations into dramatic healing ministries have all too often come to very depressing conclusions. I am filled with anger and sadness when I think of vulnerable people flocking into vast arenas in the forlorn hope that some outrageously confident showman, who, for most of them, is just a dot in the far distance, will somehow release the power of divine healing into their lives. I wish every blessing on those who have genuine healing ministries, but I pray that God will convict all who know in their heart of hearts that they are frauds, preying on the same kinds of crowds that inspired such practical compassion in Jesus. It is difficult to imagine a more terrible, devilish cruelty than offering the certainty of healing to sufferers when that promise is nothing but a lie and an illusion.

The truth about healing is so easily obscured. I have contributed to this obfuscation many times and have always felt like kicking myself afterwards. Someone tells me that her brother's friend's first cousin has been healed of an incurable disease, and I smile and nod vaguely because it feels unkind and uncomfortable to question or contradict what is being said, even though everything in me is saying that no miraculous healing has been involved.

And, you may ask, what is so terribly wrong with vague agreement? God gets the glory, and we're all a bit happier, surely. What's the matter with that? Well, the blindingly obvious fact is that God doesn't want the glory for a miracle that he didn't do. Thank him with all your heart for recovery from illness or any other good thing that happens, by all means, because all good things come from him anyway, but let us not play even well-meaning games with the supernatural power of God. The kind of pathetic response that I just described has the effect of diluting and distracting from the genuine healing ministry of the Holy Spirit, and we don't want that, do we?

WHEN MY LEG IS HURTING ...

In many parts of the church, there is a vague assumption that only deficiencies in technique and approach prevent us from seeing the kind of healings that we read about in the gospels. Perhaps a little tinkering with the controls is all that is necessary. It is easy to fall into this trap on a personal level. When I came to write this section, I realised the extent to which I have done it myself lately because my leg has been in pain. At its most absurd it goes like this:

Phase one: My leg is hurting, so I ask God if he will be kind enough to heal it. He doesn't – except by the definition of our holistic friends, who would want to point out that my mind and spirit are okay, and wouldn't I agree that two out of three ain't bad? I would point out to them with some asperity that it wasn't my mind or spirit that I injured when I fell in the bath.

Phase two: My leg is still hurting, but I have remembered a book written back in the sixties by somebody whose name I've forgotten, who said that if we praise God loudly for answering our prayers even though he hasn't yet, then he will. I go quite a long way to a secluded spot and praise God loudly and at length for healing my leg. I have to get an expensive taxi back from the secluded spot because my leg is in so much pain after walking all the way to the secluded spot.

Phase three: My leg is still hurting. I recall a preacher saying that you have to "lay hold" of promises from the Bible. Good idea. I decide to "lay hold" of the promise in that bit about your father not giving you a stone when you ask for a fish. I ask for my leg to be healed and briefly remind God of his promise in case he has forgotten it. He doesn't give me a stone, but he doesn't do anything about my leg either. Not even a fish. Not so much as a sardine.

Phase four: My leg is still hurting, but I realise how silly I've been. In the gospels Jesus nearly always forgave people's sins before healing their bodies. Of course he did! On the way up to town to do some shopping, I confess as many sins as I can think of. I end up trailing dismally around the super-market, overwhelmed by the weight of my revealed sins and my shopping, not made easier by the fact that my leg keeps giving way.

Phase five: My leg is still hurting. On the way back from the shops, I realise how spiritually timid I have been in this matter. For goodness' sake! What is the matter with me? I am a child of the Most High, a dweller in the kingdom of God. I decide to take dominion over the pain in my body with all the authority at my disposal. It might have worked except that someone came round the corner just as I was in the middle of shouting commands at my own leg. Absolutely nothing I could say. Lurched home.

Phase six: My leg is still hurting, but it strikes me that Jesus was always telling people that their faith had made them whole. In his hometown he was able to do very few miracles because the locals lacked belief. I confess my unbelief and pray for increased faith. It occurs to me that I should have mentioned my leg.

I decide to give up all this getting healed business. From now on, I announce to God, I shall just trust that you will give me what I need without complaining that you haven't given me what I want. I am secretly hoping he will be so pleased by this surrender to his will that he will heal my leg as a reward. He doesn't.

Phase seven: My leg is still hurting. I ask God to disregard all previous communications regarding my leg. Let it be as though I never mentioned my leg and the fact that it hurts. A blank sheet. A clean slate. A fresh approach. A new beginning. A healed leg? Apparently not.

Phase eight: My leg really hurts. All right, I'm getting a bit annoyed now. What do you have to do to get a bit of healing action around here? Nothing I say or don't say seems to make any difference. I have to assume either that God doesn't exist after all or that he doesn't want my leg to be healed. If things don't soon improve, I might have to give in and go to the doctor ...

You may think this sounds ludicrously exaggerated and childish. Well, it is a bit, but I am afraid that it is not a million miles from the truth as far as I am concerned. How about you?

TRUTH, OBEDIENCE, AND GOD

So, having said all these rather negative things, where do I stand on the whole issue of healing? I have no doubt that there are some who, having read what I have said so far, would dearly love to break through onto the screen of my computer so that they can tell me about their own very specific and well-documented healing. There will be others wanting to describe the ministry they are involved in where hundreds of people are healed and the power of God is manifested visibly every hour or day or week or month. Please don't trouble. Despite what I have said, I do not need to be persuaded that this is the case. I welcome and rejoice in every true account of miraculous healing that I hear. Despite the fact that my leg still hurts (are you listening, Lord?) I believe with all my heart that God can heal, wants to heal, does heal, and will heal much more through his church in the years to come.

My lack of trust is not in God but in men and women, a view shared by Jesus himself, as we learn from the second chapter of John's gospel.

> Now while he was in Jerusalem at the Passover Feast, many people saw the miraculous signs he was doing and believed in

his name. But Jesus would not entrust himself to them, for he knew all men. He did not need man's testimony about man, for he knew what was in a man. (2:23–25)

I am one of these men the passage refers to, and so I know how easy it is to delude myself. All I am asking is that we should try to tell the truth.

Hear are some points that might be worth considering.

First, in the twelfth chapter of the first book of Corinthians, Paul asks the rhetorical question "Do all have gifts of healing?" thus implying that some do not. In the same chapter he lists healing as a very specific gift, occurring in the same list as wisdom, tongues, prophecy, and others. Perhaps each of us should be asking God if this is a specific gift that he might wish to give us, and if so, what we should do about it.

Second, John Wimber, for whom I had the greatest respect, was obliged by the Holy Spirit as a matter of obedience to preach about the efficacy of healing for a year. During that time none of the people who came to him for prayer were healed, and, in fact, quite a number of them died. It was only after twelve months of faithfully doing what he was told that a dramatic change occurred and 75 percent of sufferers found healing. How much do we really want to see healing in our churches? No two people will take exactly the same path, but it does look as if God is likely to demand that we take these things seriously.

Third, whatever we may say about a specific gift, or about Wimber's year-long commitment, the most dramatic and instantaneous healing that I know of occurred when a new Christian heard the Holy Spirit whisper in her ear as she sat in a meeting. She was brave and obedient enough to take the healing hands of Jesus to a friend of ours, named Jenny, who was speaking from the front, and was rewarded by witnessing a quite remarkable physical transformation.

Jenny had suffered from a chronic inflamation of the joints that had confined her to a wheelchair for several years. Many well-meaning people had prayed for her, some proclaiming boldly that she would be healed instantly. All had been wrong. On this occasion, however, in the course of a meeting that she was leading, Jenny was not just "significantly improved", nor "lifted in her spirits", nor "upheld in her suffering", but totally, unequivocally, and indisputably healed of her physical ailment. After a brief excursion to the washroom to recover from her recovery, as it were, she returned to the front of the hall and late, on her return home, lifted her own wheelchair out of the car.

Why Jenny? Why then? Why not before? Don't ask me. I don't know. What I do know is that the girl who had prayed for this miracle was not particularly confident; in fact, she was probably more amazed than anyone else by the outcome of her prayer. She simply heard the command of the Holy Spirit, and she obeyed it. That, surely, is the important lesson for you and me. If I am a follower of Jesus, I may be required to follow him suddenly and unexpectedly to a place where I have never been before, and depending on the will of God, I may or may not go there again in the future. The obedience is what counts. Look at your hands. Go on, do look at them. Are they his, or are they yours?

Fourth, and perhaps most important, as my third point illustrates, God is in charge. He will do what he will do when he wants to do it. He will heal whom he will heal. He will not heal whom he will not heal (including legs). You may study Scripture until you are blue in the face, as some colourful characters have done, and come up with the most carefully organised theology of healing that the human brain is capable of assembling. What you will never manage to do is put together a book of rules and techniques that can turn miraculous healing into some kind of measurable or quantifiable science. Under laboratory conditions it just disappears. Thank God for that, I say. I want a wise Father, not an efficient medical administrator.

As we look to Jesus, we see in the New Testament how he healed hundreds of people in the course of his ministry. There are these two passages from the gospel of Mark for a start, one in the first chapter and one in the sixth.

> That evening, at sundown, they brought to him all who were sick or possessed with demons. And the whole city was gathered around the door. And he cured many who were sick with various diseases, and cast out many demons; and he would not permit the demons to speak, because they knew him. (1:32–34 NRSV)

> When they had crossed over, they came to land at Gennesaret and moored the boat. When they got out of the boat, people at once recognised him, and rushed about that whole region and began to bring the sick on mats to wherever they heard he was. And wherever he went, into villages or cities or farms, they laid the sick in the marketplaces, and begged him that they might touch even the fringe of his cloak; and all who touched it were healed. (6:53–56 NRSV)

The healing just flowed, didn't it? Because Jesus was there, and because he cared and because the power was in him, people only had to touch the edge of his cloak and they were made better. The very air must have hummed with the possibility and prospect of healing and health. So thrilling!

The disciples had the same experience after he gave them authority to go out in pairs and have a go without him. Jesus told them to take the good news and to heal. That's exactly what they did. They came back, filled with excitement, to tell him that even the demons had submitted to them.

Is that what Jesus wants for us? Should the healing still be flowing, and if it should, how can we help to make it possible?

We don't want to mess about and play games over this. If our thinking is wrong, we want to look to Jesus to put it right. If we have become lazy and are failing to apply ourselves seriously enough to the issue, we ask Jesus to discipline us and strengthen our commitment. If our relationship with him has atrophied and become loveless, we ask him to help us regain that closeness and subsequently the compassion for others that might make healing possible. For whatever he wants, we want it, or at the very least, we want to want it. For he was and is the Great Healer.

CHAPTER 3

TELLING THE TRUTH, PART TWO

We have looked at doubt and healing in the last chapter; let's turn in this chapter to two other areas where the truth needs to be told.

THE BIBLE

In forty years of being a Christian, I have found the Bible enthralling, boring, fascinating, puzzling, annoying, relevant, bright, stodgy, irrelevant, enlightening, depressing, and invaluable. There have been long periods when I have read it systematically and, as they say, faithfully, and equally long periods when I have made scrappy, disorganised forays into bits and pieces of books that have no discernible connection with each other. There have been passages of my life when I have not read the Bible at all and others when a crowbar was required to separate me from my holy deliberations on the significance of some hyphen in Leviticus.

I suppose I am only really saying that I am a human being, a child in many ways, for worse as well as for better, and therefore my response to the Word of God is neither as consistent nor as systematic as it might be. Having said that, the Bible is a part of my life, and I think I love it. It has changed

and moulded my thinking and my behaviour, as well as sometimes led me into dealing with specific situations in bewildering and, on at least one occasion, shocking and unexpected
ways.

WISE FOR SALVATION

I am (eternally) grateful to God for forcing his truth
through the filters of the human minds that produced and
translated this great book, and I recognise, as a believer living
in the free Western world, that I am privileged to have everything from Genesis to Revelation so readily at hand. Paul's
advice in the third chapter of his second letter to Timothy is
worth repeating.

> But as for you, continue in what you have learned and have
> become convinced of, because you know those from whom
> you learned it, and how from infancy you have known the
> holy Scriptures, which are able to make you wise for salvation
> through faith in Christ Jesus. All Scripture is God-breathed
> and is useful for teaching, rebuking, correcting and training
> in righteousness, so that the man of God may be thoroughly
> equipped for every good work. (3:14–17)

"God-breathed" is an interesting expression, don't you
think? What is the nature of breath? Breath is the vehicle
of speech, essential to life, continually refreshed, invisible,
constantly on the move, something you imbibe deeply before
embarking on significant projects. The Holy Spirit inhabits
and moves through and gives life to Scripture so that even
disorganised folk like me can know what it means to breathe
the breath of God and feel all the better for it.

If you pushed me into a corner and threatened to poke me
with a sharp stick until I told you which parts of the Bible
have been most helpful to my breathing over four decades, I
would have to say that the gospels and the book of Acts have

saved my spiritual life on more occasions than I can count. When the reality of my faith seems to be slipping away, I return to the world where Jesus walked as a man all those years ago. I tag along with him and his mother and his disciples, watching the miracles, listening to the stories, hearing the preaching, and joining in with the meals. No one seems to mind me being there. On the contrary, I feel welcome. Above all, I simply allow myself to be affected by the power and personality of the man who was God, the one who, incredibly, reads these enthralling but severely edited accounts of his own ministry over my shoulder. From my point of view, that is a good place for him to be, because when I close the book and turn around – there he is.

I love the book of Acts, not least because it is what we in England used to call a "ripping yarn", an action-packed account of life in the early church, written by a man who clearly loved to write and who was passionately inspired by his subject. Doctor Luke was well aware of the need for detail in narrative, especially as a contrasting context for miraculous happenings.

The following anecdote from the twenty-eighth chapter of Acts is one of my favourites. It follows on directly from Luke's dramatic and even more detailed description of the shipwreck that interrupted Paul's journey to Rome, where, as a Roman citizen, he had demanded to be tried in front of the emperor. After running aground on a sandbar, the stern of the boat is being pounded to pieces, and the centurion in charge issues new orders. Those who can swim are to jump over the side and make for shore, while those who cannot are to use planks or pieces of the ship to keep them afloat until they reach land. In this way the entire ship's company survives the wreck.

> Once safely on shore, we found out that the island was called Malta. The islanders showed us unusual kindness. They built a

fire and welcomed us all because it was raining and cold. Paul
gathered a pile of brushwood and, as he put it on the fire, a
viper, driven out by the heat, fastened itself on his hand. When
the islanders saw the snake hanging from his hand, they said
to each other, "This man must be a murderer; for though he
escaped from the sea, Justice has not allowed him to live." But
Paul shook the snake off into the fire and suffered no ill effects.
The people expected him to swell up or suddenly fall dead, but
after waiting a long time and seeing nothing unusual happen to
him, they changed their minds and said he was a god. (28:1–6)

Great stuff, eh? Can't you just see Paul, hard at work as
usual, hair and clothes streaming with water after immer-
sion in the sea and the driving rain, his keen features vividly
illuminated by the flames of the crackling fire? He suddenly
becomes aware that a poisonous snake, frightened by the
fire, has angrily fastened its fangs into the soft part of his
hand. A hush falls as the hospitable islanders stare in horror.
They know their local snakes. Whispering together, they wait
for the venom to do its deadly and irreversible work on this
strange, intense, practical man. To their amazement he simply
shakes the creature off into the red-hot centre of the confla-
gration, where it writhes once and then dies. From murderer
to god in a matter of minutes, as far as those islanders were
concerned. They were out-of-date on one count, and wrong
on the other.

I thank God for Acts and for stories like this. They remind
me that when a life is genuinely given to God, as Paul's was,
it will be filled with as much adventure as any man or woman
could want. Of course, my adventure will not be the same as
yours. Following Jesus will bring adventures of the mind and
the spirit as well as the body. They can happen in civilised
and uncivilised settings, in peace and in war, in supermar-
kets and in slums, in prisons and in public places. And with

the promise of adventure comes the unavoidable certainty of risk, but that has always been so. It is part of the cost.

WORDS ON THE PAGE OR THE LIVING LORD?

Yes, I do love lots of the Bible. I love the stories and the history and the poetry, and the breadth and depth of the message it contains, but I would hate to get silly about it. Do people get silly about the Bible? Yes, I think it does happen. There is a trap that all of us Christians are liable to fall into, and that is the temptation to become single-issue fanatics, homing in on some isolated aspect of the faith with almost neurotic intensity. It can happen with just about anything. I have met people, for instance, who are so distracted and excited by ideas associated with the end times and the fulfilment of prophecy that they think and talk about nothing else. At its worst, this mania is driven by the same appetite that feeds on the occult. Dangerous for them and monumentally tedious for me.

The business of healing and deliverance has fascinated and absorbed one or two church leaders to the point that they have allowed themselves to become involved in bizarre and excessive activities that are too unpleasant to mention here and have no place in the kingdom of God. Genuine healing ministries grow out of a Jesus-centred faith, not the other way round.

With others, the unhealthy focus can be their own spiritual leader. Many of the letters that I receive are from people who invested all their trust in one person, often the head of a church, and are now devastated and left faithless for a time by the discovery that their human idol has, at the very least, feet of clay.

In the case of those who have developed tunnel vision in relation to the Bible, the problem is rather subtler and more complicated, perhaps because the line between enthusiasm and obsession is such a narrow one. How, you may ask, can the Bible, the very Word of God, ever be elevated to a higher position than it deserves? The answer is very simple. In the final analysis you and I will not be saved by the Bible. It will be no use taking out a large black book with a floppy cover when we arrive at the gates of heaven and then attempting to use it as a passport to paradise. I fear that a lot of people are going to find Jesus disappointingly uninterested in technical exposition or theology. Not even the least of the angels will be impressed by our long-winded, complex perorations on the significance of the first quarter of Matthew's genealogy of Christ. It will be too late by then. There is only one way into heaven, and we hear about it from Jesus in the tenth chapter of John's gospel.

> Therefore Jesus said again, "I tell you the truth, I am the gate for the sheep. All who ever came before me were thieves and robbers, but the sheep did not listen to them. I am the gate; whoever enters through me will be saved. He will come in and go out, and find pasture. The thief comes only to steal and kill and destroy; I have come that they may have life, and have it to the full." (10:7–10)

There we are. Jesus is the gate, and whoever enters through him will be saved. No matter which path we take, we arrive at the same place. Salvation is about relationship. It has to be real, and we must not allow ourselves to be distracted from this truth by those who have become so exclusively immersed in words on the page that they have lost sight of our living Lord, the living Word, the one whose flesh-and-blood body must still exist in the mysterious place that we call heaven.

In the fourteenth chapter of the same gospel, in what is for me one of the most moving moments of the New Testament, we find an even more explicit statement of the truth.

"Do not let your hearts be troubled. Trust in God; trust also in me. In my Father's house are many rooms; if it were not so, I would have told you. I am going there to prepare a place for you. And if I go and prepare a place for you, I will come back and take you to be with me that you also may be where I am. You know the way to the place where I am going."

Thomas said to him, "Lord, we don't know where you are going, so how can we know the way?"

Jesus answered, "I am the way and the truth and the life. No one comes to the Father except through me." (14:1–6)

The Bible is not a person of the Trinity. It is the God-given means by which men and women and boys and girls can learn that God loves them and was willing to sacrifice his Son so that they can come home to him and live with him forever. It doesn't matter whether its cover is black or green or pink with yellow spots. It can be in large print or small, and the more intelligible the better. The chapters and verse divisions are very useful, but they were put there by human beings, not by God. Like the Sabbath, the Bible was made for us, not us for it, and we thank our heavenly Father for such a wonderful gift.

The clear, straightforward words of a hymn by Christopher Idle sum it up very well.

> *How sure the Scriptures are!*
> *God's vital, urgent word,*
> *As true as steel, and far*
> *More sharp than any sword:*
> > *So deep and fine,*
> > *At his control,*
> > *They pierce where soul*
> > *And spirit join.*
>
> *They test each human thought,*
> *Refining like a fire;*
> *They measure what we ought*
> *To do and to desire:*

For God knows all—
Exposed it lies
Before his eyes
To whom we call.

Let those who hear his voice
Confronting them today
Reject the tempting choice
Of doubting or delay:
For God speaks still—
His word is clear,
So let us hear
And do his will.

THANKS AND PRAISE

Here is a fourth area in which telling the truth might be helpful. I have come relatively late in life to a genuine desire to thank God from the bottom of my heart for just about everything. The theory has certainly been there for decades, and I have always believed that thankfulness is important, but for many years I don't think I had any real idea of what it means. In this passage from Ephesians, Paul clearly implies that such an attitude is possible:

> So do not be foolish, but understand what the will of the Lord
> is. Do not get drunk with wine, for that is debauchery; but
> be filled with the Spirit, as you sing psalms and hymns and
> spiritual songs among yourselves, singing and making melody
> to the Lord in your hearts, giving thanks to God the Father
> at all times and for everything in the name of our Lord Jesus
> Christ. (5:17–20 NRSV)

Giving thanks at all times and for everything sounded and still sounds a pretty tall order. In fact, stated as plainly as this, it sounds absurd. Saying thank you for the good things that happen seems much less of a problem, but are we really supposed to greet illness and disaster and bullying and cold coffee and mosquitoes and people who walk slowly in front of you on narrow sidewalks and tripe soup and impatient publishers and nervous breakdowns and utter despair with expressions of gratitude? Surely not.

Yesterday, when I had finished my daily thousand words for this book, I spent an hour and a half hunting for a cheque that had come the day before so that I could put it in the bank. I went through the same jumbled pile of papers on the kitchen table three times with minute care but found no trace of it. By the time my wife came home, I was in the process of pulling my study apart, a frazzled, sweaty, irritable wreck of a human being. My wife found the missing cheque immediately. It was not missing at all. It was in the pile of papers that I had so carefully gone through three times. My response was not a gracious one, to say the least. Should I have been grateful to God for the increase in my blood pressure, and should Bridget have thanked him very much for the snarling savagery with which her instant solution of the problem was greeted? Not in this house.

When, as has happened to us, our car collides with the only other car in the county in the middle of nowhere with four tired, hungry children in the back and there is not so much as a cottage within miles, should we feel a glow of appreciation for being allowed to partake in the glorious experience? I don't think so.

When we visit people who have been bereaved, are we to suggest to them that their predominant emotion should be thanks for the loss of a loved one? Of course not.

When wives are beaten by their husbands, should they be grateful? No. Let's not be silly.

Early verses in the book of James include an equally uncompromising and apparently impossible injunction.

> Consider it pure joy, my brothers, whenever you face trials of
> many kinds, because you know that the testing of your faith
> develops perseverance. (1:2–3)

Pure joy? Is the man mad? Is he seriously suggesting that persecutions and beatings and stonings should be a cause for unadulterated celebration? What is he talking about, and if he is in fact sane, how on earth are mortal men and women ever to be capable of such a thing?

So there is the question. How are we to give thanks for everything? I know that Paul's words must mean something, because they have been allowed to appear in the Bible, but I am also increasingly aware that God is sane and kind and practical. He would never ask us to pretend that feelings are happening in us when they are not really. What are we to do?

GOD WITH US

Well, the answer to the conundrum must surely lie in understanding what thanks or gratitude to God might really mean, and I must begin by saying that I have found one clue in my own experience of being a professional writer. Only a clue, remember, but it might help. The "professional" part is important, by the way, because although what I am about to say does have a general application, it tends to arise from the experience of those who are putting words together on a full-time basis.

For me, living in the everyday world as a writer involves a strange mixture of objectivity and subjectivity. I react to most of the things that happen in my life on two levels. The vast majority of folk will readily understand one of these, the subjective level. Something happens. We respond. Thoughts and feelings spring from our collision with the event or experience as sparks fly from an anvil or dust from a carpet. We laugh, we cry, we yawn, and we sigh. All good, natural stuff.

Since beginning to write for a living, however, I seem to have developed a quite separate and markedly different perception of the world. It runs in parallel with the one I have just described and, rather oddly, at exactly the same time. Let me give you an example.

Many years ago I wrote briefly about something that happened when I was on holiday in Denmark with the family. One day we went to one of those theme parks that offers lots of different rides and activities for children. Bridget went off with our oldest son to do a "mum with oldest son" thing, while I took the other three on a trip down a fast-flowing river in a little round boat. From the beginning this boat felt ominously unstable. Despite stern warnings from me, the two boys started to rock their bodies and lean down backwards towards the water until, at a point where there was a curve in the river, the boat overturned and my two sons, my four-year-old daughter, and I were thrown into the water. At this time I was still a non-swimmer, and simply being under the water induced an immediate panic. To make matters worse, my body had somehow become trapped between the rim of the overturned boat and the bank of the river, so that I was unable to reach the surface to draw breath.

I was terrified. Unless I fought free, or someone else helped me, I was likely to drown. I had no idea what had happened to my sons, but because they are strong swimmers, I hoped and assumed that they would have reached the bank with no difficulty. What about Kate? A dreadful knot of ultimate sadness seemed to tie itself around my insides as I speculated on the fate of my darling little daughter.

All of these reactions, the panic, the fear, and the weight of sadness, were perfectly normal ones. The other reaction, the one that happens on that objective level I was talking about just now, was completely different. You may find this difficult to believe, and I don't blame you, but it is quite true.

Down there in the damp darkness, with the weight of all these things pressing on me and no visible prospect of a solution, a very distinct part of my mind was coolly assessing the potential of this situation for eventual use in a literary context. Perhaps a magazine article, or a story that would make some telling point when I was speaking to a group somewhere. Possibly the whole thing could be adapted and absorbed into a fictional project at some point in the future.

The little man with a notebook who lives at the back of my head scribbled busily away, noting with interest the various nuances of panic and fear, the exact sensations that accompany drowning, and the emotions evoked by the imminent loss of those whom you love. He was just on the point of starting a new piece under the heading "First Encounters with God" when I managed to struggle free from my trap. I arrived, gasping, in the life-giving air, to discover that all three of my children were safe, thank God, and the industrious little man nodded interestedly as he flipped over his page and began a new one entitled "The Anatomy of Relief".

As far as I am aware, my spontaneous feelings were not and are not in any way diluted by this objectivity. It is just that my mind seems to have trained itself to be interested, absorbed, and mentally engaged by anything and everything that happens to me, whether those things are good, evil, tragic, hilarious, or just plain tedious (tedium can be electrifying, believe me!). When I apply these observations to my writing, I am, hopefully, able to reproduce the responses that occur on a normal level, purely because that heartless little man in my head has taken such comprehensive notes.

My point is that I am beginning to feel a little bit the same about the way that Jesus walks and works in this world. Things happen to us. Wonderful things. Terrible things. Ordinary things. I react to them like any other human being, but I am just beginning, with predictable lapses, to understand and believe something that rescues me from always finding myself a helpless victim of any of those things. Do you remember these words of Jesus from John's gospel?

> "I have told you these things, so that in me you may have peace. In this world you will have trouble. But take heart! I have overcome the world." (16:33)

Worth meditating on, is it not? Do take time to read the verses that precede the passage as well. This deceptively simple message from God is one that might make a real difference to you and me and the rest of the modern church if we can begin to grasp the staggering height and depth and breadth of its significance. Let us just remind ourselves of what it does not say. It does not say, "In this world you can expect to avoid trouble, because I have overcome the world."

No, on the contrary, Jesus is actually saying that we can definitely expect trouble but that we should be greatly encouraged by the fact that he has overcome the very world into which that trouble will come. He obviously does not intend this to be a contradiction in terms, so what does he mean? I believe he is communicating the potentially life-changing truth that there is not a single incident in the lives of his followers that he does not inhabit and monitor and have ultimate control over, even at those times when darkness and distress are all that we are able to see and feel.

If this is so, and as I have already said, I am just beginning to feel the truth of it in my heart, then we see that it is indeed possible to thank God in all circumstances, however grave. Jesus has overcome the power of those circumstances to shatter, or even to dent, the part of us that is safe and saved in him. From this perspective it is even possible on occasion to take the same fascinated view of our lives as that little man who scribbles in my head. What will the Lord do in *this* hopeless situation? How on earth is the Holy Spirit involved in the mess that I face today? What is the creativity of God doing with the bleak darkness that envelops me at this moment? I have no idea, but like the psalmists I will tell him just how unhappy I truly feel, and I will also thank and praise him that I am not alone and undefended on this troubled earth.

OUR ATTITUDE OF GRATITUDE

On the afternoon before writing these words, I was involved with a seminar at the Christian Resources Exhibition, which meets annually at three different sites in the United Kingdom. I was interviewing a friend named Geoff Lackey about the work and ethos of the Christian Healing Centre that he runs at Crowhurst near Battle. It had been a good session. My role was simply to put forward all the obvious questions about healing that most people would like to ask. Geoff's much more difficult task was to respond honestly to my questions. He did exceptionally well, avoiding the ever-present cliché trap and openly acknowledging that he was not able to answer one of the questions when that was the case. Shortly after the seminar had ended, a lady asked if she could speak to me for a moment.

"We've just found out that our grandson is suffering from a serious neurological illness," she said. "What I wanted to ask you was whether you think we should accept that and get on with helping him as much as we can, or should we pray for God to do a miracle and heal him?"

Foolish as I often feel when people ask me questions about the best course to follow, I had no doubt on this occasion.

"I think you should do both," I replied. "Accepting something doesn't mean that you applaud it or like it or want it or stop praying against it; it just means that you're facing the truth and getting yourself ready to do anything that needs to be done. There may be all sorts of practical help that your grandson will need. There's no point in denying what's happening to him if you want to be part of supplying that help. At the same time you can be praying from the bottom of your heart for Jesus to heal him. Responsible caring and prayer never cancel each other out. God is in charge, and he will do the right thing. Be glad about that."

Forgive me for labouring the point, but do you see what I am trying to say? That lady had clearly experienced shock and fear and deep concern about her grandson's condition, and it was right and healthy for her to express it. We do not thank God that someone we love is suffering from a debilitating condition. Why would we? We do thank God, though, that through prayer we are able to place this and all other situations within his control, knowing that he will support our work and hear our petitions. If there is to be a miracle, then the best possible thing will have happened. If there is not to be a miracle, then the best possible thing will have happened, however dreadful and ridiculous that may seem at the time. Thank goodness that the one with the power is also the one with the love and the ability to make fine judgements.

If you still find it difficult to accept this proposition, and I quite understand that you might, then it is worth considering the life of Jesus as it is recorded in the gospels. Jesus clearly displayed a wide range of human emotions. He was angry, he was sad, he was compassionate, he was amazed, he was frightened, he was hurt, he was appreciative, he was shocked, he was horrified, he was disappointed, and he was deeply moved. I sometimes hear people talk about "the human side of Jesus". A nonsense, of course. Jesus did not have a human side. He *was* human. He was true man and true God, not some weird hybrid of the two. Impossible for us to understand, but no less true for that.

These human, heartfelt, subjective responses existed in the Son of God and were inextricably intertwined with all the power and the insight and the prophetic utterance and the special knowledge that were essential elements of his divine identity. Thus we see that despite all the negative events and experiences that he had known in his life, Jesus, who had only just dried his eyes after an emotional encounter with Mary, was able to stand outside the tomb of his friend Lazarus and offer thanks to God for *always* hearing his prayers.

> So they took away the stone. Then Jesus looked up and said, "Father, I thank you that you have heard me. I knew that you always hear me, but I said this for the benefit of the people standing here, that they may believe that you sent me." (John 11:41–42)

The pattern set for us by Jesus is a reassuring and inspiring one. He felt what he felt, and he had no intention of denying it. At the same time there is a sense of vibrant excitement and anticipation in his approach to difficult or challenging situations. The wine has run out. Someone's servant is sick. A little girl has died. The authorities are viciously critical. Endless numbers of sick people drain his energies from sunrise to sunset. His cousin is executed. The sight of Jerusalem reduces him to tears. A dear friend has died and is in the tomb. One of his closest disciples denies knowledge of him. He is betrayed by the kiss of a friend. In all these circumstances his Father never fails to hear his prayers, and for that he is thankful. As we have just seen in the passage from John's gospel, allowing people to know about our "attitude of gratitude" is a means of drawing them to faith. If we could emulate Jesus in this, our lives and the lives of others might be turned upside down.

DEFAULTING TO PRAISE

I stand by all that I have said about giving praise and thanks to God, but I do believe that there is an even greater depth to be explored in this context. The writer of Psalm 8 uses the following words, words that are quoted thousands of years later by Jesus in Matthew's gospel:

> From the lips of children and infants you have ordained praise.
> (Psalm 8:2; Matthew 21:16)

Jesus said that if we want to enter the kingdom of God, we must become like little children. If we do, we shall discover that we shall be honest with our pain and default to praise, because, in the final analysis, that is the way we are made. This is not just about singing songs and saying prayers in church-related situations. It is about all that we are and will be. It is about abandoning ourselves, letting ourselves fall into an ethos or atmosphere in which the vast thing that is feebly contained within such terms as praise, gratitude, and thanks is as natural and as essential as drawing breath.

G. K. Chesterton, a hero to so many Christian writers who run out of words, said it so much better than I can ever hope to do in his book *Chaucer,* published in 1932:

> There is at the back of all our lives an abyss of light, more blinding and unfathomable than any abyss of darkness; and it is the abyss of actuality, of existence, of the fact that things truly are, and that we ourselves are incredibly and sometimes incredulously real. It is the fundamental fact of being, as against not being; it is the unthinkable, yet we cannot unthink it, though we may sometimes be unthinking about it; unthinking and especially unthanking. For he who has realised this reality knows that it does outweigh, literally to infinity, all lesser regrets or arguments for negation, and that underneath all our grumblings there is a subconscious substance of gratitude.... This is something much more mystical and absolute than any modern thing that is called optimism, for it is only rarely that we realise, like a vision of the heavens filled with a chorus of giants, the primeval duty of praise.

Thanks be to God.

My Encounters with the Safe Jesus

SLEEP PARALYSIS

I am in my mid-twenties. We are living in Bromley. I am at teacher-training college, and my wife is teaching at a local girls' secondary school. It is the early hours of the morning. I am in bed. Bridget is asleep beside me. The horrible thing that has haunted me for years is about to happen again. I am terrified. I know exactly what will happen because the details are always the same. I seem to wake but find that I am completely unable to move my body. A terrible pressure, a black, coffin-like weight, is pressing down on my chest, making it very difficult for me to breathe. A whirlwind of intense terror takes possession of my mind. A roaring sound fills my ears. I feel as though I am clenching my whole being so tightly that something must eventually explode. Desperately I strain every muscle to turn and wake my wife, but I cannot move so much as a little finger. This has been happening on and off since I was seventeen. I dread it. I loathe it. It is like a concentration of evil. It frightens me more than anything else I have ever known.

The next morning I pull myself together and visit the doctor. I am a little nervous. In the decade or so since they first began, I have never talked to a doctor about these night attacks. He listens sympathetically and tells me this is a recognised phenomenon that is known as "sleep paralysis". There is not much more to be said. I suspect that putting a label to the condition doesn't actually bring him or me any closer to understanding what it is, but there is a definite comfort in knowing that I am not alone in suffering from it. I thank him and leave.

The thing I did not tell the doctor, because I did not want him to think I am mad, is that I have discovered only one way to escape the clutches of this invisible monster. It is the name of Jesus. When the attack is at its most intense, I begin to say his name over and over again in my mind. It is as though the repetition of this name massages the evil out of my system. In these little nighttime battles Jesus fights for me and wins. I hate my sleep paralysis, but, being a person of such variable, sometimes fickle faith, I value the reality, the vividness, and the immediacy of this experience.

I suspect that when I am older and these attacks happen much more rarely, I shall find myself wishing that I had told that doctor about the power of the name of Jesus. No doubt I will hope and pray that he has found it out in some other way.

A TWENTY-POUND NOTE

It is the mid-eighties, and Bridget and I are setting off to drive up to Oxford from Hailsham. We shall be lucky if this oil-guzzling old car of ours reaches the junction at the end of the road we live on, let alone our distant, coldly theoretical destination. We can only hope, pray, and argue now and then over the route.

This is a difficult time in our lives. Because of a stress illness, I am no longer working, and we have three children and a mortgage to support. Nothing is as simple and straightforward as it was. We have very little money and only the cloudiest idea of what the future might hold. All we know for sure is that we have asked God to allow something real to happen in our lives. We don't want to mess about anymore, we have said. We want to follow Jesus. No doubt these are the rash and ignorant prayers of children, as we have no real concept of what an answer to our petitions might mean, but they did seem to penetrate the ceiling of the kitchen for once, and they did come from the bottom of our confused and desperate hearts.

Our trip to Oxford is in connection with the fact that I have been doing quite a lot of writing during the last year or so. Apart from anything else it has been a good therapy for me. Taking the dark things from inside and placing them in the light has had a good effect on the way that I think and feel, and the daily discipline of putting pen to paper has had a steadying influence on my approach to daily living. For some time now Bridget has been posting off examples of my writing to a variety of publishers and magazines, hoping that someone might think them worth offering to the public. Generally the response has been disappointing. Perhaps because I am writing out of such chaotic personal circumstances, the pieces I produce do not fit easily into the normal style of evangelical literature. In fact, one or two publishers have been very arch and sniffy indeed, informing me in brief, terse letters that they are sure their readers "would not like to have the Lord Jesus Christ spoken of and about in this manner".

Rejection is not easy to handle at the best of times, let alone at a juncture in your life when everything in you is continually expecting to be rejected anyway.

Then, quite recently, something different happened.

A couple of years ago, Bridget met the American writer Elizabeth Sherrill during the recording of a series of short television programmes made by TVS, the company that held the franchise for broadcasting in the south of England at that time. The names of John and Elizabeth Sherrill are, of course, well known to millions of readers across the world because of such immensely successful Christian bestsellers as **The Cross and the Switchblade**, **God's Smuggler**, and many other titles.

Elizabeth, a genuinely modest, charming lady, suggested that Bridget and the other programme participants should feel free to send her examples of any new writing that they had specially enjoyed. Two years later, remembering this conversation, Bridget decided, a little nervously, to do exactly that.

Elizabeth's reply arrived a fortnight later. I was in bed but awake when the postman came. Bridget was downstairs. There was a short pause after the noise of letters thudding onto the front-door mat, followed by the sound of Bridget's feet on the stairs.

"Read this," she said, holding out two sheets of paper.

It was the kind of letter you dream about. Elizabeth's encouragement was warm and overwhelmingly positive. As far as the question of my writing was concerned, it has had the effect of lifting me above my swamp-like pessimism, not just on that one morning, but in the days that have followed. Being believed in by people you respect seems to do wonderful things for the soul.

A few days after the arrival of Elizabeth's letter, we had a telephone call from a man called Ray Cripps, who introduced himself as an old friend of the Sherrills. Ray had been told about the exchange of letters and was ringing to invite Bridget and me to visit him in the small village near Oxford where he lives with his wife, Jean. After a lifetime of involvement with books and publishing, he was keen to lend us a few useful books and perhaps offer some advice.

Now we are on our way to meet him. We arrive at last in the attractive village of Whitney. After our usual tension-filled process of oscillation, we manage to locate the house where the Cripps live, and pull up outside in a cloud of oily smoke. The front door opens as we step out of the exhausted car. Ray is at the door and turns out to be a quiet, good-natured elderly man with very kind eyes and a faith that is as natural and as unobtrusive as breathing itself. Jean is an even quieter person than Ray, but she welcomes us with great friendliness.

We very much enjoy our time with Ray, who has much of interest to impart and suggest. We feel very comfortable and well looked after. On leaving he presents me with a number of books that might be helpful to me as I pursue a career that, realistically, is still purely hypothetical. We have said our good-byes and are actually sitting in the car with the engine running when Ray comes up to the window on my side. He is holding something in his hand.

"Take this," he says, holding out a twenty-pound note.

I am paralysed for a moment. Ray has obviously detected that we are far from being financially ebullient. Twenty pounds is a lot of money in 1985, and an even more significant sum for Bridget and me. We never have any extra money. After putting enough petrol in the car to get back to Hailsham, we shall have about fifteen pence to our names. The provision of extra, unexpected money has its own peculiar piquancy. Should I take it?

Yes. It is a simple act of kindness. Take it and don't start babbling.

I thank Ray, and we drive away. As our pillar of smoke chugs southwards I reflect on the fact that some kind of circle has been completed. Bridget wrote to the Sherrills. The Sherrills contacted Ray Cripps. Ray invited us to his home and encouraged us. There is a twenty-pound note in my hand. We will be able to buy food and other essentials for the children when we get back. But it is far from being just about the money. It is about something much more important. The circle is the circle of the community of Jesus. Perhaps our prayer is already starting to be answered. My new prayer is that when the opportunity arises, I shall be as ready and willing to part with twenty pounds as Ray has been.

Arriving home we realise how much richer we are than when we left this morning.

TRAVELLING MERCIES

I am travelling in a train with my young son Matthew on the way to Norwich in East Anglia to join the rest of the family. Over the last couple of weeks, rain has fallen torrentially all over England. Flooding has created problems for many people in low-lying areas, and the sheer force of water falling from the eternally overcast sky has been quite awe-inspiring at times. I am more aware than ever that we British are never prepared for extreme weather conditions, even, strange as it might seem to outsiders, when they involve rain.

Matthew and I have enjoyed our journey so far, talking and playing games and reading and eating and watching things through the window. Now, though, the train has stopped. In fact, it has been at a complete standstill for some time in what appears to be the middle of nowhere, and no one seems to know what the problem is. There is an indefinable bleakness about sitting in a silent, stationary train in the middle of a field. It feels like being part of a picture in a book illustrating a chapter that deals with hopelessness, or lack of motive and meaning.

Finally, the guard announces the disturbing news that the train is unable to move either forwards or backwards along the line because the ground beneath the tracks has given way in two places, one in front of the train and one behind, the result of constant rain soaking into the bank that supports the twin railway tracks. We are stranded. For me, this information results in a gloomy sensation of instability. Suppose the ground immediately beneath the train were to give way? Our carriage might topple over. There would be severe damage. People might be injured or even killed.

On the other side of the carriage, a girl is sitting. I would say that she is in her late teens, but I am not terribly good at ages. She looks as though the news has, very understandably, left her feeling quite disturbed. I wish I could offer her some support, but suddenly being befriended by a strange man on an isolated train in the middle of a field might be the last thing she needs at the moment. Then, as I look at her, a conviction grows in me that this girl is a Christian. I cannot think how or why I should know that this is the case, but I cannot escape the strength of this feeling. Should I ask her? If she is a Christian and I tell her who I am, she might remember that I write books and feel reassured and a little safer. If not, she will begin to believe that being stranded in this train is the least of her problems.

I run out of nerve. Instead of asking her the question directly, I start to hum Christian choruses to myself, just loudly enough for her to hear and recognise them if I am right about her being a believer. The look Matthew gives me suggests that he thinks I may have become seriously unhinged.

But my cunning plan works. The girl recognises the tunes. Her eyes light up. She speaks to us. She is a Christian. When I mention my name, she knows who I am and seems quite relieved to have companions in this tense situation. Matthew and I sit with her until the time comes for us to climb down from the carriage and walk back along the track to a point past the damaged tracks on the southern side of the train. Here, another train has arrived to rescue stranded passengers and take them to a mainline station from which they can reach their destinations by a roundabout route. When we arrive there she phones her parents to tell them what has happened. Matthew and I phone Bridget in Norwich to explain why we are going to arrive so much later than we had planned. We part from the girl at this stage in our travels and wish each other well for the future.

Settling back into the corner of the carriage for the next part of our long journey, I look back over the last couple of hours and decide that all things really do work together for good, even if it takes a few chicken-hearted, badly hummed choruses to do it.

RESTORING THE BALANCE

It is nearly time for Evensong, and I am taking a breath of air outside one of the oldest university chapels in this part of England. I am to preach here tonight. Soon the chaplain will come out and indicate to me that the time has arrived for us to process into the chapel and take our places for the service. I tend not to do a great deal of processing in the normal run of things, so, although a little daunted, I am quite looking forward to the formality of the ceremony. Meanwhile, for one who has been feeling as tense as I have recently, the opportunity to breathe in the rich magic of an early autumn evening feels as healing and useful as anything I would be able to get on prescription.

Men, women, and children are still filing in through the west door of the chapel, but one lady approaches me and, having gained my attention, stands very four-square in front of me, looking directly into my eyes. I take stock of her. She is probably in her mid-forties, and she appears to be dressed from neck to toe in several layers of dun-coloured wool, with a rather unexpected bobble-hat on her head that is striped in three or four virulently bright colours. There is an open Bible in her hand and a smile on her face that instantly makes me feel uncomfortable. I have seen this sort of smile before. It is the consciously kind but concerned, predatory smile of one who is probably planning to say something "in love". I prepare myself inwardly and try to smile back in a cheery, casual way.

"Hello," I say with as much brightness as I can muster.

Her smile widens like a bowl of custard filling up towards the brim, until she overflows with a yellow tide of heavenly serenity and God-given authority.

"Do you believe in the Lord Jesus Christ?" she asks, still looking me steadily in the eye.

"Er, yes," I reply feebly, gesturing towards the chapel, "I'm just about to preach at the service."

She shakes her head, humbly dismissive of the idea that this puny fact might constitute or even imply any kind of convincing argument.

"Do you believe he died on the cross and rose again so that your sins could be forgiven?"

"Well, yes, I do. I am a Christian, so I –"

"His Word tells us that he is faithful and just to forgive us our sins. Do you know that in your own life?"

She is referring to her open Bible as she speaks.

"Of course I do. I –"

"And we learn in the book of Revelation, do we not, that the Lord Jesus Christ stands at the door of our lives and knocks? Has he been knocking at the door of your life, and have you allowed him in to sup with you?"

"Yes, I have. I just told you that I am a Christian."

I am wasting my time. I know I am. It is as though the words I say pop and vanish like bubbles blown from a wand before they have a chance to reach her ears. I brace myself and try not to imagine reaching out and grabbing the bottom of her woolly hat in both hands. What pleasure it would give me to pull it down over the roguish smile that has now appeared on her face.

"Do you want the Lord Jesus in your life? He would have you allow him in, you know."

I open my mouth to say something in reply but close it again as I change my mind. What is the point? I am unlikely to convince her that I am a Christian by shouting at her or suffocating her with her own hat. Glancing at my watch, I mutter something about having to go now and walk away towards the door into the chapel. I am really angry with her, but more so with myself. It has happened all over again. Why do I let these people get to me with their silly little set-piece speeches and their soupy smiles and their utter refusal to hear anything that is said to them? Why did I not just stop her in mid-flow and protect the peace I need for what I am about to do? I feel really upset now. There is and probably always will be a little part of me that, despite everything that has happened, is all too ready to doubt my relationship with God. Bobble-hat would love to be privy to this juicy piece of information.

Lacking total assurance, eh? Ah, very significant! She would fire Scriptures at me like bursts of shrapnel over that one.

As I walk into the space at the back of the chapel where the choir is assembled and ready to enter, I am feeling quite agitated. How can it be possible that someone going on and on at me about Jesus like that can make me doubt my own competence and fitness for doing something similar but (hopefully) different with this congregation? I speak to Jesus in my mind and ask him to calm me and guard me during the service. I feel woefully out of balance.

All of a sudden a lady leaves her seat in the chapel and slips out into the area where I am waiting with the choir. I have never seen her before. She smiles at me, puts a folded piece of paper into my hand, and then hurries back to her seat. I am not able to look at the contents immediately because it is suddenly time to process into the main chapel. I manage to unfold the sheet of paper, however, and read it sinfully and secretly during the second hymn. It is a note of appreciation. The lady who wrote it has been through terrible times in her personal life and has been helped to retrieve and retain her faith in Jesus by reading books that I have written. Hearing that I was speaking locally, she had been hoping for a chance to give me her letter this evening. She is not asking for any further acknowledgement of what she has written; she just wants to encourage me.

I am overwhelmed. Christmas in autumn. Once again I thank God for the Body of Christ, for Jesus among us, bringing strength to parts of the body like me, who are weak and continually in need of being shored up against the effects of our own deficiencies. I finish the hymn with several times more gusto than before.

The hymn ends. It is nearly time for me to speak, and the balance, thank God, has been restored.

BEHIND THE BLANK STARES

I am dying on my feet. I have been speaking for nearly half an hour, and most of the assembled company have the same blank stares on their faces as they have had since about three minutes after I started. I am not used to this. Most of the people who come to my talks are smiling even before I begin. They feel they know me through my books and are already geared up to enjoy the event. Not here. Not tonight.

The evening began badly as far as I was concerned from the moment I walked through the door. For some reason the organiser had failed to mention the dress code for the evening. All the people present except my friend Ben and me are wearing dinner jackets and bow ties. In itself that doesn't matter, of course, but it is disconcerting to feel like a chicken at a penguin convention.

The evening began and has continued until half an hour ago very pleasantly as far as everyone else is concerned. Every single thing not involving me has gone really well. They enjoyed chuckling and guffawing and exchanging news over drinks before dinner was served. They loved their four-course dinner when it came. They had great fun with the chairman's report, which was peppered with in-jokes and satirical references to many of those present, and they adored roaring out the club toast, which, I gather, is always drunk at these yearly general meetings of their club. They must be a little puzzled about the rest of the agenda. Why has someone they have never heard of been maliciously imported by the chairman to ruin such a wonderful evening by imposing thirty minutes of dull nonsense on them?

By now my top lip is sticking immovably to my teeth, but I lack the composure to stop and take a sip from the glass of water on the table beside me. I know it would go wrong if I did. I would probably choke and spray water over those nearest to me. Or else I would put the glass back down on top of the end of a spoon and it would overbalance and spill all over the tablecloth and my neighbour's knees and he would feel obliged to say it didn't matter.

To make things worse, a violent pulse has started to throb in my left thigh. So insistent is it that I feel sure my entire being must be visibly vibrating. My whole body seems to be closing down. Perhaps I have actually died. Yes, maybe I have missed out on heaven by a technicality, and now I am doomed to deliver the same boring material repeatedly to people who want nothing more in the world than for me to shut up and sit down so that the nice fun stuff can begin again. Hell for them and worse hell for me.

How has such a dreadful situation arisen? It has arisen for the following reason. This year's chairman of the organisation in question happens to be not only a clergyman but also a Christian, a fatal combination. He felt it would be good for his members to hear a more overtly spiritual message than they were accustomed to, and clearly he genuinely does want to be a part of helping as many people as possible to find Jesus. It is true that I sometimes speak to groups who are not church-based in any way, and in the main these talks have gone quite well. Encouraged by such memories I agreed to come. Now I wish that on this date I had been unavoidably committed to some easier and more congenial and relaxed task, building a full-sized model of the Empire State Building out of matchsticks whilst riding a mechanical rodeo bull, for instance. This has been an unmitigated disaster. All I want is to fill my allotted space of time and then clear off as quickly as possible.

I steal a glance at the large clock on the opposite wall. Three minutes to go. These one hundred and eighty seconds last for something approaching a week, but at last my ordeal is over. My final little pleasantry is received as though it were an obscure mathematical equation delivered to a group of innumerate depressives, and I sit down like a sack of pulpy potatoes dropping into a box. The end of my talk is greeted with much body-shifting and volleys of previously withheld coughing and throat-clearing, together with a patter of applause, fuelled mainly by relief, and prolonged a little way past its natural life span by goodwill, politeness, and a sort of dulled compassion. The chairman stands and thanks me for my talk, which, he claims, has been much enjoyed by all the members. All the members try, with varying degrees of success, to look as though they concur.

I feel utterly wretched and downcast. On a purely personal level, I am reminded once more of how fragile I actually am when it comes to this standing up and speaking business. No matter how much success I may enjoy, failure still has the power to chew me up and spit me out. Not for the first time I draw a crumb of sustenance from something my friend Stewart Henderson, a fine poet, said to me many years ago: "All gigs pass." And they do—even this one.

It isn't just the personal aspect, though, I think to myself, as people start the process of getting up and fetching coats and shaking hands with everybody before setting off for home. I came here hoping that Jesus would be visible in some helpful way to at least some of these people. All they got was a leg-quivering, dry-mouthed bore who must have made his faith sound like the most dismal thing on earth. So depressing. I don't even have the heart to embark on one of my defensive self-justification exercises.

Several people wish me a polite good night in passing, but I am suddenly taken aback by the fact that one man has stopped abruptly on his hurried journey to the door, leaning right in towards me so that his mouth is close to my ear. The passion and vehemence of his very private communication reminds me of one of those film scenes where a prisoner risks his life by passing essential information to the outside world.

"You are never going to know," he whispers with urgent intensity, "what this evening has meant to me!"

And then he is gone.

I can most accurately compare the sensation resulting from this briefest of encounters to a moment on a freezing cold day in New Zealand when, with ecstatic gasps of relief, I slipped my shivering, bathing-suited body into one of those outdoor hot spring pools.

Such relief indeed after such despair. I may have been useless, but Jesus certainly was not. I have no idea what the situation has been or is with the man who whispered in my ear, and I do not need to know. I am just glad like a child. I sit down again, a little weak in the knees, and thank God for the great privilege of being an idiot for him.

I add, however, that I am not sure my nervous system can handle many such privileges in the course of one year. All gigs do pass, but I have a feeling that the flavour of this evening will linger on my tongue for quite some time.

HOME OR FORTRESS?

It is eight o'clock in the morning on the fifteenth of April. In the last half hour I have stumbled out of bed, had a shower, got dressed, and fulfilled my duties in accordance with our strictly enforced "last one up makes the bed" rule. Now I am standing at the south-facing bedroom window, gazing out across miles of green fields towards the far horizon, where, in a haze of soft spring sunshine, ancient Pevensey Castle looks more like a cleverly tinted sketch of itself than the real thing. Pevensey Castle was the model for C. S. Lewis's Cair Paravel in the Narnia books, and we take a childlike pride in having it on "our" horizon.

I am well aware of the next two items that appear on my official, if unwritten, agenda. The first will be breakfast, probably a bowl of Crunchy Nut Cornflakes, and the second will be writing another thousand words of this book. But I can't. I simply can't. Apart from the fact that I am not sure what I ought to write about today, this is the morning I have been waiting for, ever since a first faint rumour of spring reached the air of southern England as long ago as early February. It is as though someone has been up all night frantically cleaning the world. The scrubbed, cloudless sky must be as sublimely blue as God ever intended it to be, and there is a rippling excitement in the air, first cousin perhaps to the thrill we know when someone we love and have missed finally comes home.

I can do my thousand words later—maybe. All I need to do now is bulldoze Bridget into colluding with me in avoiding work. I doubt she will take too much bulldozing. As I descend the stairs, I move into brisk, let's-get-on-with-it mode.

"If you're ready," I call out over the banisters, "we might as well get going now."

"Get going where?" asks Bridget slightly worriedly from the kitchen, perhaps feeling that she has forgotten some previous arrangement.

"To the Exceat, of course," I reply. "We'll take the dog for a walk out by the river and then go back to the café and have a huge pot of coffee and a pile of croissants. Are you ready?"

I was right. She hardly takes any bulldozing at all. On the contrary. We don't often take the morning off, but she agrees that it would be a sin to waste this one on sensible things. Within minutes we are in the car, Lucy the dog is hanging over the backseat, paws crossed like an old man leaning on a fence, one bat-ear up and the other down, panting with the excitement of an impending walk, and we are on our way to one of the most beautiful spots in this beautiful county of Sussex.

Come to the Cuckmere Valley one day, if you can. I'll show you where it is. When you do come, make sure that you walk out towards the estuary beside the river that winds in convoluted loops through flat, grassy land towards the sea. That is what we are doing now, slightly warily, because there are a lot of sheep around here, and our good-natured, year-old Welsh border collie has not been exposed to the real thing before. Since coming to live with us, Lucy has made repeated, optimistic attempts to herd our two cats into corners of various rooms in the house, but their strenuous objections to being randomly cornered by this upstart of a newcomer have not encouraged her. What will she do out here? Dogs who chase and worry sheep are, quite rightly, very unpopular with farmers.

We need not have been alarmed. Lucy takes one nervous, sideways look at these large woolly creatures and decides that they are best left alone. She decides to wait and have another go at corralling those cats when she gets home.

Our walk over this sun-swept land of grass-carpeted chalk and flint is blissful, despite the fact that we are both suffering aches and pains in legs and backs at the moment. At one point we spot a heron, loitering with aristocratic ease at the edge of the water, waiting for his lunch to swim by. He spots us and, still without undue haste, lifts his majestic wings and sails with effortless grace to the bank on the other side of the river. A light breeze is chasing hordes of excited little ripples across the surface of the water as we turn and make our way back to the Exceat café where our late breakfast awaits. This place too is a dream. The tables are set in a warmly inviting, brick-floored courtyard, enclosed by the rough old flint walls that are so typical of this area. I love it here. An important part of me seems to relax whenever we come to this spot.

As we approach the entrance to the courtyard, I become aware of another couple heading in the same direction. He is a slightly built man with a handsome head of grey hair. He limps quite heavily with one leg as he walks. His wife or companion is darker in complexion. She has a friendly, birdlike face. They enter the café area just after us. We four are the only people there. Bridget and I are seated at one of two tables that are positioned on a slightly elevated area. Lucy is sitting by my feet. At ten o'clock in the morning, this corner of the courtyard is bathed in gentle April sunlight. I watch the couple as they settle themselves at the table next to us. Before finally lowering himself into a chair, the man looks around at his surroundings for a moment and utters a sigh of sheer appreciation.

"Goodness me!" he exclaims in a light, pleasantly cultured voice. "We are so *very* lucky, aren't we?"

This remark seems to be addressed to me as much as to anyone else, so I agree with him. I have always liked people who are appreciative.

"That's right," I reply. "All things being equal, what more could you want than this place on this fine morning?"

We all smile at each other. These smiles of ours are the slightly rueful, benevolently thwarted smiles of people who feel that they really ought to know each other well but cannot quite bring themselves to abruptly leap the more formidable social fences that traditionally divide those who have only just met. There is something else as well, though. I know that this man wants to talk to us. How do I know that? Body language? Instinct? Something else? I don't know. I could be completely wrong. We shall see.

Our coffee and croissants arrive. The coffee, darkly entombed in a pot twice the size of the one they usually give to two people, is a Kenyan blend. It is rich and hot and strong. Perfect. The croissants are fresh and buttery and served with extra butter and marmalade. I positively shiver with pleasure. Can perfection be cubed?

Our neighbours are then served with their breakfast. Unfortunately, the young female waitress trips as she nears their table and virtually throws the contents of her tray onto the table and into the laps of her customers. It is like a scene from a comedy programme. Confusion reigns. Everyone is more concerned for the waitress than for themselves or their breakfasts. The place is positively awash with civilised behaviour. Eventually order is restored and all is well. But it was a unifying moment for the other couple and us. I really do think that this man wants to talk. We shall see.

The grey-haired man's companion begins to speak to him about family matters. I eavesdrop shamelessly. Clearly she is his wife. She speaks at considerable length without a pause, and he pays full, polite attention to what she says. Nevertheless—I just know that he wants to talk to us.

She comes to the end of her remarks, and he immediately turns to us and makes a genial comment about our dog. Everyone likes Lucy. She is a child and a clown, a genuine enthusiast. It is a good way to begin. In the course of the conversation that follows, we learn that the man and his wife have never been here before. They live twenty or so miles away in a small town that we know a little, mainly by passing through it, but recently for a quite different and very specific reason.

Both of these people are teachers. In addition, he makes stringed musical instruments. They work in the local branch of an educational establishment that was founded many years ago by a man with a comprehensively developed philosophy about the teaching of children and indeed about life itself. We tell them that we are close to one individual who benefited enormously from this educational system in the past but that we know very little about the broad philosophy lying behind it. I ask them if there is a Christian element in the teaching of the founder. They both assure me that there is, but as these two delightful people enlarge on this point, I perceive that there is a broad chasm between their understanding of the Christian faith and mine. I can see Jesus in what they are, but I cannot find him in what they say. Not for the first time, I find myself wishing that life could be simpler.

The man goes on to tell us that there can be healing properties in the instruments he makes, and he shares his experience of making a lyre for a cancer sufferer who was subsequently healed as he held and played the instrument in question. His wife joins in with enthusiasm. There is a distinctly evangelical edge to the way in which they are speaking now. For us it is a novel thing to be "reached out to" by people with a different but very distinct way of thinking and believing. We listen to all that they say, nod interestedly, and make little comment.

What our breakfasting neighbours do not know is that I have been recently asked to speak at an outreach meeting next year at the village hall in the little town where they live. The person who invited me has already pointed out that a number of folk from the school where these people work will almost certainly be coming along. I reflect on the fact that there is a more than fair chance of this couple being present on that night. I will Bridget not to mention that we are Christians involved in full-time ministry. I learn later that she is willing exactly the same thing in my direction. The motivation for this restraint is the same for both of us.

Next year, if these two people do come along to the village hall to see what is going on, it would be nice if they could recognise us and remember that we listened to everything they had to say when we met by chance, without launching into a diatribe based on our own activities and beliefs.

They leave before us, and although our parting is very genial, we once again endure that instant of baffled silence that occurs when strangers wish that they could become friends but cannot quite shorten the process to fit the circumstances. How silly we are. Never mind—I have a feeling that we shall be seeing those two people again.

It is in the car on the way home that Bridget expresses her relief that neither of us talked about our faith or the work we do. She is absolutely right, of course. There is a time for saying these things and a time for keeping our mouths shut and listening to others. I have got it wrong (both ways) so often in the past. For instance, there was a time when the situation we were in just now would have elicited a different and very predictable response from me. I would probably have felt the need to meet another person's expression of faith and philosophy with a very clear and possibly rather strident statement of my own. I fear that for less than honourable reasons, I might then have proceeded to tell that person about my writing and speaking career, just to show them what a significant character they were dealing with, as it were. Ludicrous but true, I'm afraid.

As we drive up through Jevington towards Polegate, we ask ourselves what the difference is between then and now. Bridget suggests, and I think it is true, that in recent years Christianity has become much more of a home than a fortress for both of us, and especially for me. It is where we live, where we belong and have a place. We can go in and out and visit all sorts of other places because we know that we shall always return to our home at the end of the day. There is no longer a need to act in an aggressively defensive manner when we are confronted by ways of thinking that are different from our own. I guess this must be much more useful to Jesus, who can use our obedience to reach a world of prodigals, but is often obscured by the rather ugly wall of defiance that tends to be thrown up when we feel threatened.

I suppose it is all about safety. Are we safe in Jesus? Bridget and I decide that we are more secure than we were but that the fortress mentality is still a part of us and needs to be resisted. Meanwhile, we pray that we will always know when the right time has come to defend our faith. We are still talking about these things when we arrive home and park in front of the house. We are home. It has been a spectacularly lovely way to start the day, but something tells me that it was not exactly a morning off.

"I still haven't worked out what I'm going to write about today," I say to Bridget as I unlock the front door and Lucy bounds in to hunt for the cats.

Bridget stops and thinks for a moment.

"Why not write about what happened this morning?" she suggests.

"Good idea," I reply. "I will."

And I just have.

PART TWO

TENDER
JESUS

Thoughts and Reflections on the Tender Jesus

CHAPTER 4

TURNING THE WORLD UPSIDE DOWN

As I sit here this morning and begin this new section on the tender Jesus, I would like to do four things that seem very important. The first is to remind you of a Bible verse that I am sure you already know well. Second, I would like to tell you about something very disturbing that I witnessed recently. Third, forgive me, but I am afraid I am going to offer you a piece of advice. I am sure you are as humbly prepared to accept it from me as I would be to accept a similar offering from you. Fourth, I want to introduce you to a friend of mine. Finally, I shall try to explain why all of these things fit with each other. Oh dear, I suppose that's five things. Never mind. They are here because when we put them together, they will help us to understand how the tenderness of Jesus can enter into our lives in the most unexpected ways and from the humblest quarters.

THE VERSE

Okay, to start with then, here is the verse, and it comes from the nineteenth chapter of Matthew's gospel.

> "But many who are first will be last, and many who are last will be first." (19:30)

Got that? Good. Don't do anything with it for now. Just keep it in the back of your mind until later. Thank you.

THE EVENT

Now we come to the recent disturbing event. I was involved in a big Christian conference held in one of our smaller English cities, the name of which is not even faintly important to the story I am about to tell. The conference was spread over a week, and it utilised venues all over the city, each one offering a different seminar or activity group or opportunity for worship. As well as doing my usual late-evening presentations (I have come to the conclusion that I am too grindingly, unremittingly serious to be anything but humorous at most public events), I had been asked to contribute four or five minutes to one of the two big worship sessions at the beginning of the week. The venue for this occasion was a rather beautiful old-fashioned theatre, rich in golds and reds and curly carved wooden bits, ideal for such close cousins as vaudeville and Christian services. As the time for worship drew closer, there must have been close to a thousand people making their way into the building, buzzing with anticipation as they filed along the rows to take their seats before settling down in readiness for the evening to begin.

I was sitting in the middle of a small group up on the platform, a position I have never enjoyed occupying very much. It makes me feel exposed and foolish. I have sometimes imagined that there might be a huge question mark sitting in the air above my head, a visible summing up of the query that must be in the minds of all those present: "Who on earth does he think he is, perched up there like some big fat canary who thinks he's got something important to chirp about?" Inverted vanity on my part, do you think? Perhaps. I think it might have more to do with that squirming, toe-curling sense I frequently have that the size and tidiness and apparent assurance of these big Christian events can leave mere human beings feeling rather small and useless. I remember meeting a lady after an evening meeting that had featured a very popular and persuasive speaker.

"What did you think of it?" I asked.

"Oh," she said, her eyes lighting up, "it was wonderful, and he was fantastic, a really good speaker, but ..." She sighed, smiled resignedly, and shook her head. "It's not for me."

I frowned.

"What do you mean it's not for you?"

"Well, I'm just ordinary," she replied. "When I get home there'll be the washing up to do and the clothes to wash and all that. You know what I mean, kitchen-sinky stuff. I'm just ordinary."

"But look," I said, probably sounding a little frantic because I had found what she said so upsetting and I suddenly realised I might never see her again, "if it's not for you, it's not for anyone. Not me, nor the man who was speaking tonight, nor any of the other people who were there. Don't you see? Jesus came to die for you just as much as he did for anyone else, and—and he finds things like washing up and looking after people really important. In the very best of ways, he was a very ordinary sort of fellow himself." There was a pause as I ran out of things to say. "Oh, please don't think it's not for you ..."

She thanked me very nicely, but as she hurried away into the darkness towards her ordinary life of service to others, I could tell she was far from convinced. I prayed that God would meet her somewhere else. He probably will. He seems to be endlessly ingenious when it comes to that sort of thing.

I digress. Sorry. I was sitting on the platform among the other contributors, waiting to do five minutes when my turn

came. The evening began with announcements, then proceeded through singing (accompanied by one of those bands
that battles to remain on the sane side of berserk), a drama,
one or two interviews, more singing, my bit, a Bible reading,
and more singing until it was time for the talk. The speaker
for the evening was an extremely well-known man. By that I
mean, of course, well known in Christian circles. He walked
with impressive calm up to the lectern at the front of the stage,
gripped its edges masterfully with both hands, rested one foot
on the raised base, and surveyed the expectant congregation
much as Moses might have surveyed the multitude from the
mountain. A hush fell.

"When you arrive at the gates of heaven," he began, his
stirring tones, enhanced by the soft transatlantic accent, ringing round the packed theatre, "and God says, 'Why should I
let you in?' what will you say?"

The congregation froze, of course, as many Christian congregations tend to do at such moments. Their expressions
said it all. It was going to be one of those talks. It was going
to be one of those excruciating addresses where you know
you're unlikely to come up with the right answers to any of
the speaker's questions, and you'll probably end up deciding
that you never really were a Christian after all and you might
as well give up and just wait for hell's gates to clang shut
behind you forever.

I fancied that I could almost hear some of the hysterical
inner responses to the speaker's question.

"I dunno! I dunno! I dunno what I'll say! I'll say—I'll say,
'Squirrel!'"

Building on the dramatic tension created by his initial question, the speaker went on to tell the congregation exactly what
they should say to God at the gates of heaven. The formula
as prescribed. All good stuff, of course, in itself. Repentance,
forgiveness, redemption, salvation, the works. The congrega-

tion listened, taking mental notes in the hope that they might get it right next time. The speaker paused and, after another Charlton Heston-style, 180-degree panning survey from the slopes of the mountain, began to speak once more.

"If," he announced with grave authority, "you did not answer the question I asked in the way I have just described, then you are probably not saved."

Depressed, fearful silence. The congregation seemed to congeal and consider. Had they answered the question in that way? Well, had they? Had they got it slightly wrong? Missed some vital detail? Messed it up completely by saying, "Squirrel," instead of quoting John 3:16? Were they saved? Or not? Or what?

I cannot possibly know for sure how those thousand Christians felt. I can guess, though. My guess is that a significant number of them trailed back to their hotels and boarding houses and self-catering apartments with a sad sense that as things stood, there was no question of anything but failure and rejection awaiting them at the gates of heaven.

Now in many respects, I have the same feelings about Christian speakers as most other people, even though, mysteriously, I am one. At their best they–that is, Christian speakers–can be enormously helpful and inspiring. At their worst they might be boring or, deadliest of all, harmless. Boring speakers do at least create a space in which I can think without being disturbed. Harmless ones make me inconveniently cross. Generally speaking, though, we assume that they are all coming out of the same camp, as it were. Sitting on that platform, however, I reflected on the fact that I had recently begun to see how mindlessly we swallow ideas and declarations that may be useless or flawed and damaging. You know how it is. An outside speaker comes to your church and, after the worship has ended with a dying fall, begins his talk with a dramatic statement. Perhaps something along these lines:

"The New Testament is not, first and foremost, about love; it is essentially about faith."

Then he stops and stares at us, daring us not to agree with him.

Well, yes, we all think in vague desperation, sounds reasonably all right. Love, faith, that sort of thing. Sounds as if he knows what he's talking about.

The fact is, though, that if he had begun his talk by declaring earnestly that the New Testament is essentially about love as opposed to faith, it wouldn't have made a scrap of difference really. Faith, love, things like that. Must be pretty well on message, surely? Christian congregations are, in the broad sense, so sure that they know nothing and that the speaker probably knows everything that they will sit like baby birds, waiting for juicy, nutritious truths to be dropped into their beaks. I hesitate to say this, being a Christian speaker myself, but you can get away with murder when you're the one standing up at the front. As long as you sound confident enough and are able to pause dramatically, quote Scripture, and induce guilt in appropriate measures at well-chosen moments, it is unlikely that anyone will question what you actually say.

These reflections on the danger of becoming too accepting of speakers came to a head when I saw the effect that the "Gates of Heaven" speech was having on all those people at the conference. It hit me quite suddenly, busily engaged though I was in the important business of trying to hide behind somebody in the chair in front of me, that this man was, to put it impolitely, talking nonsense. I asked myself what I would say to God in the unlikely event that he meets me at the gates of heaven and demands to know why I should be allowed in. And there was no problem. Absolutely none. I had no doubt about the words I would use. They came to my mind instantly. "You *love* me," I would say, sounding like a child having a bit of a joke with his daddy. "You *know* you do!"

I would back my theology against his. How about you? Try to imagine me staring into your eyes like Moses Heston from the mountain, daring you to disagree with me.

Seriously, though, when I next meet that man, I shall, if I am feeling brave enough, tell him what I thought of his talk. I shall tell him that I have probably done similar things in the past, but, I shall add, that fact doesn't make it right. I suspect that he, being well defended and intellectually able, will, with all Christian restraint and tolerance, endeavour to make nonsense of what I have said and then go and think very hard about it. I hope he will not react in a negative and defensive way. I hope he will eventually agree with me and apply to join the "I'm useless but God loves me" club, an organisation to which I and many others find it very useful to belong.

THE ADVICE

So that was the recently witnessed event, and now we come to the advice that I promised. It is quite simple really.

If you truly wish to follow Jesus and be welcomed into heaven by him when your life comes to an end, you must make sure that you mix with important and influential people. This is absolutely crucial. Don't listen to what anyone else says. If you waste your time hanging around with no-hopers, you must not be surprised to find that there is an aura of chilliness around the gates of paradise when you arrive. Have you got that? Stick with people who will do you a bit of good, rich people who inspire respect and admiration and have some real clout in the places where it matters. Very important. Don't say I didn't warn you. End of advice.

Never mind for the moment what your initial response might be to that last paragraph. Store it and your reaction away for now with the Bible passage and the disturbing event, and we'll come back to all three of them, I promise. Hear me out, please.

THE INTRODUCTION

So now we come to this very good friend of mine whom I want you to meet. I have been so looking forward to writing about this. Goodness me, what can I tell you about him, and where shall I begin?

I first became aware of this extraordinary man more than twenty years ago, when Bridget and I moved with our three young sons into a tall, thin Victorian house on a pleasant, shady street at the south end of the town of Hailsham in Sussex. Soon after settling in we discovered that a straggling procession of slightly unusual looking people passed our house every morning on their way up the hill to a large building at the top of our road. This building, it transpired, was a work centre that catered to men and women with learning difficulties, a section of society that until recently had been labelled "mentally handicapped". A neighbour told us that the residential home in which these people lived was on the other side of the big, grassy recreation ground at the bottom of our road, a facility that was to occupy our three sport-loving boys for vast tracts of every spring, summer, and autumn as the years passed in our new home.

Our observations of this daily procession suggested that the hostel staff must be in the habit of staggering the departure of their residents in order to avoid the possibility of one big group crowding along the pavement all at the same time. There would be little groups of three, generally and intriguingly in exactly the same position in relation to one another, presumably because they found security in familiar, repeated patterns. Mostly, though, they walked in pairs, often holding hands. One of these duos particularly interested all of us. These two men walked at precisely the same speed with a strictly maintained distance of what we estimated to be four good paces between them. The one at the back grumbled loudly, incessantly, and incomprehensibly in the direction of the one in front, while the leader of the mini-procession kept his eyes fixed widely and immovably on the path before him as he mumbled a far less forceful but equally unceasing and unintelligible defence. We never did manage to pluck up the courage to ask what the argument was about. We doubted that either of them would have known anyway.

There was one man who always walked on his own.

In some ways this fellow was more bizarre in appearance than all the others. He was probably in his mid to late thirties, in fact roughly the same age as me, as I was to discover later. He was tall, very tall indeed, probably about six feet five inches, although a stoop and a tendency to walk with slightly bent knees reduced the impression of height a little. Exceptionally thin with enormous hands and feet, it was as though all his strength and energy had gone into growing these extremities, leaving little over for the development of his body. My feet are large, but this man's shoes were easily into the size 15 to 16 range, while his hands were the hands of a fairy-tale giant.

His head was disproportionately large as well, and he wore spectacles in which each lens really did look like the bottom of the proverbial wine bottle. Because of the massive magnifying power of this pair of glasses, his eyes were huge and staring, like the twin orbs of some puzzled deep-sea fish peering blankly out from the inside of an inadequately proportioned bowl. His dark hair was long and unkempt, as was his beard. As far as we could tell, seeing him from day to day, his clothes were uniformly too small for his body, trousers at half-mast, pullovers clutching his waist, each jacket sleeve ending somewhere between elbow and wrist.

I was especially interested in a stiff red folder that this very singular person carried under his arm as he made his tottering, spidery-legged way up to the training centre each morning and then back again for the return trip in the late afternoon. I managed to make out that it had the words "POET MARTINI" written in large, uneven capital letters on the front. There was something fascinating about the care with which it was clasped against the skinny body by one of those vast hands. Clearly the contents of this folder were very precious.

I seemed to see a lot of this character as the months went by. Eventually, no longer working because of illness, I had a lot of free time on my hands. I would often pass the strange man with the red folder as I walked along the street, or I would see him stalking slowly past our house as I sat at my desk in our upstairs sitting room. In those early days of inactivity, I was spending hour after hour up there by the window, gazing out across the road, or nosily checking out which of our neighbours left their houses when and for how long. I was doing my best to come to grips with a novel activity called "writing", which was proving to be quite therapeutic and might possibly fill a few of my empty days until a proper job came along.

I never spoke to the solitary man when I passed by him on the pavement, and he certainly never appeared to be aware of my existence. In any case, I doubted if his eyesight was good enough to see anything more than a couple of feet from his face. Despite this total lack of meaningful contact, something important was beginning to grow – in me, that is.

I had been doing a lot of appropriately childlike praying and thinking and dreaming as I sat in my eyrie overlooking the street each day. Perhaps as a result of this, there was a new and refreshingly untutored willingness in me to look for

Jesus being alive and at large and imminently active in the things and people that surrounded me. Was this in some way responsible for the way I began to feel about the man with the folder? I don't really know. What I do know is that a conviction began to grow in my heart or my mind or wherever convictions take root that Jesus wanted me to get to know this man.

Let me break off here for a moment so that I can tell you exactly what I mean by that. One of the things that used to drive me mad when I was reading those wonder-filled testimony paperbacks was the way in which "supernatural" events were described, explained, and referenced within the boundaries of an exclusive language that consistently failed to touch genuine human experience at any point. This left me either puzzled or intimidated. What was the writer talking about? Why did it all seem such a mist to me? Perhaps I just wasn't spiritual enough. It happened in services and meetings as well. When, as an embryonic Christian, I tried to ask questions about these things, the response made me feel that I must be breaking some unwritten rule. Mind you, even then the fact that this hypothetical rule was unwritten seemed a bit of a giveaway. We really do have to try to move away from needless obfuscation and simply tell the truth until we run out of words. At that point there is absolutely nothing wrong with saying that an experience is beyond description, but this is very different from wrapping it up in language that God himself would have trouble comprehending.

So what exactly do I mean when I say that I thought Jesus wanted me to get to know the strange man who walked up and down our road each day?

After all that I have just said, I feel like chickening out now. Pathetic, isn't it? Could I not say that the Lord touched my spirit and then move quickly on to the next bit? No? Oh, all right then. It was something like this:

I felt a growing intensity of interest in the man with the file under his arm, and the pressure of this finally reached a point where I was experiencing something akin to mental discomfort about my failure to engage with him in some way. Odd but true. Perhaps because I was spending a lot of time trying to talk to God and read the Bible during that period, I tended to automatically place all the things that were happening to me (this one included) within that context. As soon as I made a mental connection between my attitude to the man in the street and the proposition that God was or wanted to be involved in every aspect of my life, a sense of what I can only describe as "rightness" pervaded the whole situation and left me with one crucial question: What was I going to do about it?

That, as nearly as I can perceive and express it, is the anatomy of my conviction that making contact with this man was a matter of obedience, and it interests me to see these words on the page. They illustrate a key aspect of Christian living that crops up repeatedly in this book – the need to set one's mind to the place where there is always an expectation that God will be involved and creative and active. It is well worth emphasizing this act of the mind and heart because, for me at any rate, it can make all the difference between vibrancy and dullness in the life of faith.

Take the experience of being stranded in a railway station, for instance. Instead of finding it annoying and boring, I might become intensely curious about what God will do with this unexpected and, in human terms, unwelcome extra and empty half hour, or however long it is. I am cheating a little, because I love being stranded just about anywhere, but I'm sure you get the point. The problem with this, and it is a perennial one for me, is that I slip out of the habit of making the right mental adjustment and forget that God is not just in the picture but is in charge of the picture. It is worth working on, though, because daily life in the context of an omnipotent God with really good ideas can be quite exciting.

Anyway, where was I? Ah, yes, the big question. Filled with the knowledge that I ought to make contact with this chap whom I had mentally christened "Martini Man", what was I going to do about it? Well, I can tell you exactly what I did about it. Filled with a growing certainty that God wanted me to do something – I did nothing. That is what I did about it. I did absolutely nothing. Nil. Zilch. I wanted to do something, but I kept losing my nerve. He looked so strange, you see, and I worried about what he would say if I broke into his huge-handed, plodding, folder-clutching world for no other reason than that, prompted by my religious delusions, I wanted to feel more comfortable with myself and my Creator.

Weeks passed. Still I did nothing. Still I watched from my lofty perch as he walked up to work in the morning and paced slowly back down the path on those hydraulic knees each evening. Still I felt uncomfortable. Like a silly kid, I tried to console myself with the reflection that all the business about God and Christianity might ultimately turn out to be a load of garbage, in which case no one would ever care whether or not I had taken the trouble to make contact with some stranger in the street. This is a common mental ploy of mine in matters of sin and disobedience, but it never works and it never had the slightest chance of making any difference this time.

More weeks passed.

At last the day arrived when I am tempted to assume that God, perhaps reverting to his more Old Testament persona, must have decided to sort the thing out once and for all. It was about nine o'clock in the morning, and I was sitting at my desk drinking coffee as I cast an inward eye over the things that I might write that day. Outside, the long, leafy street that ran so appealingly between dignified rows of tall

Victorian houses appeared to be deserted. Then a slight movement caught my eye. I leaned forward across my desk to get
a better view. Fifty yards down the road, a man was lying in
the gutter, apparently unconscious but twitching visibly, as
though in the grip of some kind of fit.

(I am sorely tempted to say that this incident occurred
directly beneath my window. It would have made a much
neater story, but it would not have been true. I remember
Professor Roy Peacock very honestly admitting that he had
to make himself go back and rewrite one section of his testimony book because he had concertinaed three divine happenings into a much shorter space of time than was actually
the case. I know how he felt. Always tempting but never a
good idea. I have just mentioned this point to my wife, but
she pointed out that if the collapse in the gutter had happened immediately beneath my window, I would not have
been able to see it because of the hedge separating our front
garden from the pavement, so I could be selling God short. I
have added this very good point at the risk of extending this
parenthetical paragraph to such a length that you will have
the greatest difficulty in remembering what was happening
before it started.)

Next to the figure in the gutter lay a red folder, from which
loose papers had detached themselves and become spread
across the path in oddly pathetic disarray. My heart seemed
to rise into my mouth. It was him. It was the man with the
huge hands. For some reason he had collapsed and obviously
needed immediate help.

A picture formed in my mind of God standing beside me,
arms folded, one eyebrow raised, tapping the toe of one foot
on the floor. "Well," I imagined him saying briskly, "either
get up and do something, or let's forget it altogether. What
do you think?"

Well, that was that, of course. No more messing about now. No more prevarication or cowardly retreats. The time had come for me to do something. And I did. There was no stopping me. Without a moment's pause I called my wife. There are times when marriage is vividly revealed to be the blessed state that it actually is.

After quickly phoning for an ambulance, we made our way down the road and knelt beside the prostrate figure, unable to do much more than murmur vaguely comforting things and collect his papers together. When the ambulance arrived at last, we hung around on the periphery of the action, making those anxious miniature miming movements of lifting and carrying as the ambulance drivers did the actual work, and then, quite suddenly, he was gone, whisked away to the general hospital in Eastbourne.

The next day I looked up the number of the hostel and rang them to find out if they knew how the patient was doing. I learned that the man with the folder was called Paul and that he suffered from intermittent and extremely severe epileptic fits. That was what had happened to him the previous day. The fall in the road had left him with some cuts and bruises, but other than that he was doing well in the hospital and would be back home in a couple of days. Leaving my name and address, I thanked them and put down the phone.

Three or four days later, someone from the hostel phoned to ask if it would be all right for Paul to come round that evening so he could thank us for helping him. I made all the statutory oh-it-was-nothing-really-it-wasn't noises and agreed that six o'clock would be a good time for Paul's visit. Punctually at six a tall, thin shadow darkened a tall, thin section of the glass panel in our front door. It was Paul, still clutching his red folder under one arm. He had to duck slightly to walk through our old-fashioned doorway.

Now, I said earlier that we need to avoid needless obfuscation and tell the truth until we run out of words. I am glad I have already said that, because I find I run out of words as I face the task of trying to explain what it meant to me when Paul first came into our house. What I can say to you is that it was as though Jesus himself had walked through our front door. This man, this very special gift from the tender heart of God, available to me when I at last responded to the Holy Spirit with obedience, has enriched my life immeasurably in the two decades since I first began to enjoy the privilege of knowing him. He is, quite simply, the nicest, warmest, most loyal friend I have ever known, and since that first proper meeting, he has visited our house on a Wednesday or Thursday evening every week, other than when illness or holidays make his visits difficult or impossible.

As Paul began to visit week by week, we learned many things. He is a poet, a musician, and a man with great compassion for the victims of this world. He displays a rare gift for appreciation of people and jokes and just about any other good thing that comes his way. The folder under his arm was a collection of his poems, some bad, some good, and a few very good indeed. At that time he was calling himself the "Poet Martini", a variation on Martin, his middle name, hence the inscription on his folder. Over the months that followed our first meeting, we were able to fill in quite a lot of our new friend's history.

Having suffered brain damage at birth, Paul grew up with a variety of what were then called mental handicaps, as well as the condition that is known as Giantism, which explains his extreme height and the excessive growth of feet, hands, and head. As a small boy he was fortunate. He went to a very advanced boarding school, where children with learning difficulties were encouraged to develop skills and talents in a way that was unknown in most special schools. He was taught to speak German, some of which still remains in his memory. His accent is excellent. He learned to play the piano and the recorder and to write elementary pieces of music. He encountered poetry and loved it. He still loves it.

Finding that I was also hoping to be a writer was a matter of great joy for Paul, although, mysteriously, he doubted that I could be a poet when we first met because, as he said, "my dear sir, you have no buckles on your shoes." His own poetic output was prolific in the days when we first knew him. His poems were written on sheets of lined A4 paper in spidery capital letters, big enough for Paul to be able to read what he had written through those thick-lensed glasses.

"I write poems on every subject you can think of," he announced one day to Bridget in his soft, deep voice, "sometimes very insignificant subjects. For instance," he added in perfect innocence and without a scrap of malice, "I've written one about you."

Bridget thanked him gravely.

When my daughter, Kate, was born a year after we met Paul, he held the tiny body of my beloved girl-child in the hollow of just one of his huge hands. Gazing with amazement at the little life that was gurgling peacefully there, I am sure he enjoyed that obscure sense of flattery that most of us feel when we are allowed to see ourselves as appropriate receptacles for a new life. It was the first time he had ever held a tiny baby.

On two occasions Paul has suffered his violent epileptic fits in our home. They are terrible things to witness, and the threat of them hangs like a perpetual dark shadow over Paul's life. One happened as he was sitting on a chair in the kitchen and was over fairly quickly. The other was much more serious and took place near the top of our stairs, a real danger if we had not heard what was happening and managed to arrive quickly at his side. I have an abiding memory of the period immediately following that second incident.

After the convulsions came to an end, Paul slipped into a deep sleep just at the spot where the fit had happened at the top of the stairs. It was impossible to move him until he came to, so I simply slipped a pillow under his head and left him to recover consciousness in his own time.

Five minutes later the front doorbell rang. It was a friend from down the road who had popped up to ask me a question about a meeting that was to be held in our house later in the week. Standing at the door with my back to the stairs, I was in the middle of explaining various details when I realised that I had lost my friend's attention. His eyes, wide and staring, were fixed on a point somewhere above and beyond my left ear. He lifted a hand and pointed a wavering finger in the direction of the landing at the top of the stairs.

"There's, er–there's a body at the top of your stairs ..."

I turned and looked back over my shoulder. At that moment one of my young sons was carefully but unconcernedly stepping over Paul's oversized head on the way to his bedroom.

"Ah, yes," I said, "I forgot for a moment. That's Paul. He's just–well, he's just having a little lie down ..."

Paul will never be able to live independently. He lacks the practical skills required for surviving on his own. At the same time he has not found hostel life easy, being a quiet person who enjoys such pursuits as conversation and classical music. Because of that his friends are important to him. When there is a gap between our meetings for any reason, he can become quite worried and nervous that something has gone wrong, that he has failed in some way and damaged our relationship. Negative patterns formed in the less constructive periods of his life are difficult to break. Fortunately, he is soon reassured.

Is Paul a Christian? I have just spent five minutes sitting here at my desk, staring out of the window, my fingers hovering over the keyboard, trying to decide whether to ask and attempt to answer this question. I have a feeling that there are some who will be unable to read what I have to say on this subject without feeling a certain disapproval. In fact, that is precisely what happened on one occasion when Paul happened to be visiting and a member of one of the local churches dropped in at the same time. This latter visitor, a graduate from what one might call the Mike Tyson school of evangelism, took me aside to bite my ear, as it were, about the fact that he found it almost impossible to understand why I had not had Paul signed, sealed, and delivered into the kingdom of God within a week of knowing him, let alone during the five-year period since then.

"Look, *I'll* tell him about the Lord," he said, as though he was offering to unblock the drain outside the kitchen door as a special favour to an impractical man.

"No, you won't," I replied with rather unusual vehemence. "It's not appropriate, and it's not happening."

I almost had to physically drag the man away from his unsuspecting prey. He went off with his unexpressed zeal coming out of his ears like steam. I hope he has forgiven me by now.

Why did I not want this spiritual enthusiast to tell Paul about his need to "get right with God"? If it came to that, why hadn't I had more to say to Paul about this Jesus who is such an important part of my life? After all, he would have gone along with anything I said. Conversion guaranteed. Easy. So why not?

Once again words grow slack.

I think it had something to do with the fact that God was already in charge of Paul. He brought him into my life and gave me his friendship as a gift. Perhaps we both gained from the relationship, but of the two of us, I had received by far the most. I had certainly told my friend that I am a Christian and had even taken him to a few church-related events, but there seemed to be, and still is, a brake in my spirit that switches itself firmly to the "on" position whenever I am tempted to railroad him into faith as I know it. Only in the most organic and least religious way have I ever felt that "Christianity" is an important part of Paul's and my knowing each other.

I remember getting terribly het up on learning that there was an entry in Paul's official file to the effect that he had been "befriended by two born-again Christians". Whoever wrote these awful words was obviously referring to Bridget and me. I pointed out with some asperity that no such horribly ugly and patronisingly predatory thing had occurred. Rather, three people had become friends because they liked each other, and Bridget and I happen to be Christians.

God will judge whether I have been right or wrong in my attitude to Paul. I shall leave it to him. If my zealot friend is right, I shall repent. In the meantime I can only express my gratitude to Jesus for the great pleasure and honour of knowing Paul for so many years.

FITTING IT ALL TOGETHER

So those are the four things that I said I wanted to mention: the Bible verse about the first coming last and the last coming first, the incident at the big Christian festival, my advice about sticking to influential people, and the man called Paul who has been such a good friend to me. How do they all fit together?

First of all, let me say I have an awful feeling that those "first and last" words of Jesus will turn out to be true.

"Of course!" you will say to me. "Jesus said them. Of course they're true!"

Well, you may say that, but there is little evidence that even those of us who call ourselves Christians truly believe them. How can it be the case, we ask ourselves, that God really has turned the world upside down? How shall we face his challenge to our fixed views of who and what is genuinely important and significant?

I have my own little list of people who will definitely be first in heaven, regardless of their status here. There are, for instance, two ladies who work with street girls deep in the slums of Bangladesh. Bridget and I met them four years ago. They will never write a paperback or speak at a Christian conference, but they are heroes of the kingdom. My mother and my wife's mother must also go on the list. Our friend Lily is another qualifier. She has gone to be with Jesus now, but her whole lengthy life as a nurse and a missionary was spent in the service of others in the name of her Master. She was wonderful, tough as old boots, fragile like lace, wise like a child, and gloriously unsung. She will have been staggered by her reception in the Golden City. Then there is the elderly man who came over to pray for me before the opening session of a recent event. I have no idea what his name is, and I shall probably never meet him again in this world, but he shone with that light which is nothing more nor less than a reflection of the source of all light and demands no acknowledgement in this world. Finally, do you recall the ninety-year-old saint in prison with Richard Wurmbrandt in Rumania, the one who was asked by non-believers if he could tell them what Jesus is like? These people had never seen a Bible and knew nothing about the Son of God.

"Well," said the old man with great courage and humility, "he is a little bit like me ..."

My list is quite short. God has a very much longer list of his own, and I am quite sure that the name of my friend Paul features on it somewhere.

These whom I have mentioned have been the last, as far as the world is concerned, and in heaven they will, to their own enormous surprise, be the first. Hence my advice to you to hang on to important and influential people, those who are rich in grace and good deeds. Stay very close to them and hope that some of their wealth and heavenly fame rubs off on you. I am shamelessly opportunistic about such things.

If, as our American friend suggests, we are likely to be quizzed at the gates of heaven about our qualification for entering, assuming all else fails I know exactly what I shall do. I shall name-drop. I shall point at my friend with the large hands and feet and the tender, accommodating smile on his face, and I shall say to God, "It's all right, Lord; I'm with Paul. I'm a friend of his."

That should do the trick.

CHAPTER 5

THE GOD WHO DEFAULTS TO COMPASSION

When you write something in a little study at the end of a hall in a smallish house in an obscure part of Sussex somewhere in the south of England, it can seem as if you are talking to yourself. The only other person in the house today is my mother-in-law, and she is fast asleep. No one else is here. Even my wife has gone out. Through the two windows of my study, all I can see are a few trees, lots of grass, a couple of thrushes, and an old ram who dreams most of his life away under the hedge at the side of the field. Surely, whatever I punch out on this keyboard will have no effect on anyone else, will it? That is how it feels. But of course I am wrong. At some time in the future, people—some people—are going to be reading my words, unbelievable as that still seems to me after all these years. As I think about the tender Jesus and how we respond to him, I am asking myself how I can say the thing that is on my mind without sounding critical to the point of being destructive.

I shall begin by giving you an example of what I mean but have not yet said.

MAKING GOD IN OUR IMAGE

When Bridget and I were living in the Midlands (for those outside of England, the Midlands is, well, in the middle of England), we once spent the day with a Christian family from South Africa who were staying in a local house belonging to a mutual friend. We enjoyed our time with them. The two children were lively, interesting people. They were polite enough to make the effort to communicate with us, but not so polite that the event became one of those awful funereal social occasions. Their parents, Jill and Frank, were relaxed, easygoing, and naturally hospitable. It was a pleasure to spend time with them. They were the kind of people with whom you felt you could talk about anything.

After a sunny, laid-back lunch out in the garden, Frank and I left the others to their own devices and settled down in the coolness of the sitting room to drink coffee and get to know each other a little better. Frank talked about the beautiful part of the world where their family home was located, not far from the southernmost tip of the African continent, and about how excited the whole family had been at the idea of coming to this country, a land whose rich history had embraced their own origins in times gone by.

Frank wanted to know if I had ever been to South Africa. I explained that I had visited that dynamically beautiful, tumultuous land on two occasions, once for a speaking tour in 1993 on my own and again in 1995, when Bridget and I worked together and three of our children came with us. I mentioned how impressed and moved I had been by the role of true followers of Jesus in the process towards relatively peaceful social and political change.

That did it. It was like throwing a switch, or as though somebody had performed one of those large-scale conjuring tricks in which one person disappears completely and another appears in his place within a split second. The new Frank, the one who had been triggered into talking about his Christianity, was significantly different from the old one. This one's eyes had lost their bright friendliness. They had become narrowed and wary. Even the physical posture was stiffer and slightly more aggressive.

Like a rocket, Frank launched into his views on God, Jesus, the Holy Spirit, the church, spiritual gifts, the right way to approach worship, the wrong way to approach worship, and several other things that I can't remember now. The whole thing was punctuated with Bible verses, neatly inserted into their appropriate supporting slots. I found myself irresistibly reminded of Gladstone, Queen Victoria's least favourite prime minister, who addressed his monarch, according to the queen's description, as if she were "a public meeting". I listened to the mixture of dogma, bits of Bible, anecdote, and fierce assertion from the man opposite me with some alarm. The conjuring trick that had metamorphosed Frank seemed to have had the extra effect of emptying my chair altogether. I had a feeling that as far as Frank Mark Two was concerned, I had become just another receptacle into which his idiosyncratic expression of the truth needed to be poured.

It was not, you understand, that Frank made any statements of fact with which I would necessarily have disagreed. How could I have aspired to such heights in any case? He obviously had a much wider and more comprehensive knowledge of the subject than I did. No, the thing I found so difficult was that the Jesus I thought I had identified in my new friend, the relaxed, clear-eyed Jesus who smiled at his children and had made me feel so welcome earlier in the day, had disappeared from the room with Frank Mark One, and I found that I really did not like this screwed-up, unattractive substitute at all.

To sum up the problem with a necessary paradox, Frank was far more Christian *without* his Christianity. And this provokes the question that I was so reluctant to put into words just now. Why does it so often happen that I like people less when they talk about their faith than when they talk about other aspects of their lives? Why do people like good old Frank become such diminished versions of themselves whenever they move into "God mode"? Why is there a temptation to leave Jesus out of the things we love and to present the world with a shrunken, sonorously moral, abstract version of a faith that is, or should be, born out of the complex, generous, fatherly love of God?

Have a look at this extract from the twentieth chapter of Exodus, the first commandment that Moses brought down from Mount Sinai:

> I am the Lord your God, who brought you out of the land of Egypt, out of the house of slavery; you shall have no other gods before me.
> You shall not make for yourself an idol, whether in the form of anything that is in heaven above, or that is on the earth beneath, or that is in the water under the earth. You shall not bow down to them or worship them; for I the Lord your God am a jealous God. (20:2–5 NRSV)

My suggested answer to the questions I have just asked is that we have as many false gods in this era as the Israelites encountered in ages past. Ours are subtler and more dangerous though, because they are disguised as the one true God, and most dangerously of all, many of them bear his name. One of the very worst and most common of the false gods is a harsh, coldly abstract, uninvolved distributor of rules and regulations that many Christians of my acquaintance are allowing to have far too much influence in their lives.

My friend Linda, for instance, is a marvellous homemaker and hostess but simply cannot accept or believe that the God she worships has any interest in the part of her life that is given over to these things. I don't know exactly who this heartless entity is, but I suspect that his sole aim is to turn the eyes of women like Linda and men like Frank away from those places where life and love and laughter and beauty and tears and disaster are to be found. Such real, vulgarly human things signal the inevitable presence of God to all those who have finally understood that the Creator of the world really did become man.

Here is the updated version of the first commandment, given to us by Jesus in the twenty-second chapter of Matthew's gospel.

> "Love the Lord your God with all your heart and with all your soul and with all your mind." (22:37)

I certainly want to do the thing that Jesus tells us to do here. I want to love God, even if I fail to do it with the total commitment that is called for by this commandment, but I am learning to be very wary of attaching myself to some twisted or distorted image of the true God. And it can so easily happen, more often than not when we fail to remember the process by which, according to Genesis, the first book of the Bible, God created humankind.

> So God created humankind in his image, in the image of God he created them; male and female he created them. (1:27 NRSV)

Problems arise when men and women attempt to reverse this process by recreating God in their own image, and I suspect that you would be able to see evidence of this happening in church groups and services all over the country on every Sunday in every week of the year. Don't get me wrong; there is a real and profitable fascination in seeing different facets of the true God revealed through the varying personalities of his followers. These variations are riches indeed. However, that is definitely not what we are talking about here.

DISCARDING WRONG IMAGES OF GOD

Another example. Sam was an ex-builder, a rough diamond of a man, who began coming along to my friend Alan's free evangelical church in Liverpool after his wife had died. Sam really appreciated the sensitive way in which Alan handled the funeral. Lonely and sad after losing his wife of forty years, he came to one or two of the Sunday morning services after that and found that he greatly enjoyed the friendliness of the congregation and the comforting feeling of having a ready-made family to belong to. Sam joined one of the weekday evening house-groups, and within a matter of months, he had made a decision to become a Christian and follow Jesus.

Sam's testimony on the Sunday morning following his decision was received with appreciation and joy by the rest of the congregation. Conversions are not so frequent in most churches that they lose their sense of novelty and excitement. It is always good to know there is something about "us" that has helped to draw a person to Jesus. Besides, there was a quality in Sam's granular, uncluttered approach to talking about his newly found Saviour that was very attractive and accessible. Over the next few weeks, Sam quite often brought a thought or a Bible verse to the congregation, until eventually he was encouraged to become part of the speaking team, contributing every two or three weeks to a prearranged teaching plan. It was shortly after the beginning of this arrangement that Alan realised things had started to go seriously wrong.

There were two aspects of Sam's teaching that Alan and the rest of the elders found increasingly worrying. One was the fact that the bright, basic simplicity of those original testimonies seemed to have disappeared altogether. In its place was manifested an uncompromising sternness, a sense that God was using Sam to tell people off rather irritably about their inability to follow all manner of spiritual rules and regulations. God does express anger, of course, at different times and in many different places, but the cross, impatient, intolerant entity that appeared to be continually lambasting the congregation through Sam was very far from being the wise, caring Father whom Jesus loved and loved to teach about.

The second feature of the change in Sam's speaking style that caused concern was an unwillingness or inability to relate his comments to the stage in the teaching plan that had been allocated to him (with his agreement) by the elders. It was very difficult. Slavish adherence to other people's ideas is one thing, but complete departure from an agreed plan is another.

Alan became more and more exasperated and frustrated by the Sam situation as the weeks went by. Easy for outsiders to say that he should simply have stopped Sam from speaking or instructed him to change his approach. Realists know only too well that church life, like family life, is never quite as simple as that. You can devise the most wonderful plans and theories in the rarefied atmosphere of your private study or in the company of like-minded others, but actually carrying out these plans can be very tricky indeed. Jesus himself was continually astonished by both the shallowness and the depth of faith demonstrated by the individuals he encountered. The smooth running of churches, like all organisations, is messed up by the presence of us annoying human beings, and I am afraid it is never going to change much on this side of heaven.

Apart from anything else, Sam's hectoring deliveries were spasmodically reinforced by soupy praise from one or two members of that peculiar church species, the "indiscriminate encouragers". Encouragement is a marvellous gift. It has changed my life more than once. Like all gifts, though, it has to be used with insight and wisdom. I would hate to have my appendix taken out by a hospital porter who had been encouraged by a colleague to believe in himself and "have a go".

By the time Alan spoke to someone outside the church about his problem, he was in a state of impotent annoyance as far as Sam was concerned, as much with himself as anyone else. It had been allowed to go on too long, and now it was difficult to see where to go with the situation. What were they to do about Sam's aggressive preaching? How should they tackle it?

"Don't tackle the preaching," suggested his confidant. "Tackle Sam. That's what it's really all about, wouldn't you say? It's not a formal church issue. It's a personal one. Get close to the old boy and find out what's going on."

It was good advice. In the course of two or three relaxed social encounters with Sam, Alan began to realise that the old widower was dealing with a fairly common problem. Perversion of conversion by reversion you might call it, if you want to be as verbally egg-bound as I am. When the euphoria of that first encounter with Jesus has passed, it is easy to allow ourselves to be drawn back into the prison of what we were and are, and to forget that by the mercy of God and because of what Jesus has done, there is no longer a need to complete the sentence imposed on us by law without grace. Sam wasn't preaching the Word of God when he stood up in front of the congregation; he was preaching the word of Sam, a harsh, punishing, inflexible doctrine, applied by himself to himself and to the things that he found when he looked into his own heart and, in his panic, forgot that Jesus had taken over the seat of power in that place.

Ironically, encouragement was just what Sam needed, not encouragement to continue using the front of the church as an opportunity to beat up himself and everybody else in public, but encouragement to believe that the initial joy he had found in Jesus was not misplaced and that his sins really were forgiven. It will take awhile, but when his confidence has deepened, Sam should find it possible and pleasurable to preach the love as well as the judgement of God.

Sam's confusion is very understandable, but we should not underestimate the potential danger of allowing people to publicly present others with a god that is largely a product of, or a reaction against, their own problems or neuroses or desires. None of us are immune from this possibility, of course. We are vulnerable human beings, and it would be foolish for any of us to claim that we have a crystal-clear view of God. But we must be watchful in this matter. I have seen so much of it, and it worries me.

The mean person who preaches a mean God.

Greedy folk who are convinced that God wants us all to have lots of money.

The woman who suffered under heavily punitive parents and finds that "the Lord" has taken over where her parents left off.

The highly organised man who hates messes and knows for sure that God is fundamentally one big, complex chart.

A person who has known rejection after rejection and has a great deal to say to nervous Christians about the ease with which we can step off the narrow way and lose our salvation.

Disorganised Christians like me who lean towards the view that there is a divine blessing on benevolent irresponsibility.

I could go on. The list is a very long one because most of us, at some point in our lives, will almost certainly fall into the trap of passing on an image of God that is more to do with us than with him. And what a lot of silly nonsense it all is. And what a waste of the truth. Because I do actually see the true God working in the real, day-to-day lives of people like

Linda, just as he worked through the dressmaking skills and general goodness of Dorcas, whose fascinating story is told in the ninth chapter of Acts. Through Linda he laughs and cares and cooks wonderful meals. He loves to make things special for anyone who walks through the door. He has sudden, fascinating enthusiasms; he cries when things go wrong with the children and rejoices when they go right. He loves and appreciates the Linda who actually is, and perhaps that is the blinding fact that she really cannot bring herself to believe.

Mind you, the sudden recognition that this has been the case can be very therapeutic. When people tell me they have stopped believing in God, I quite often have to congratulate them on finally leaving behind an image of the deity that always was a mile wide of the mark. What profit would there have been, for instance, in Sam's continuing to cringe beneath the unremitting aggression of the false and unpleasant god that he had fashioned with his own hands? Why on earth should Linda take any joy at all in the prospect of spending eternity with a miserable deity who takes no interest in her practical care for others? What profit is there for Frank in letting his God-given generosity of spirit be shrunk and diminished by the obsessionally ranting creature that crawls onto the throne of his life whenever religion is on the agenda?

No, let us be brave and move on. Let us not inflict these idols on ourselves, and certainly not on anyone else. We can cross over to new pastures of truth on the stepping-stones of our discarded images of God and do a lot of good to the body of Christ in the process.

On the wall of our church, we have a banner depicting a signpost in the shape of a cross, accompanied by the words "Jesus Christ, the same yesterday, today and forever". That statement is absolutely true, but it is equally true that the way in which we perceive him does not necessarily remain constant. The Jesus I thought I knew yesterday is not the same

Jesus that I know today, and the Jesus I know tomorrow will, by the grace of God, be even closer to the pure reality that will finally be revealed in heaven.

Having said all that, here is the obvious question: How do we avoid the idol-worship trap, and how can we learn about the true nature of God? Well, despite already having had so much to say about it, I cannot claim to be any kind of expert in this area. I can, however, offer you some ideas and reflections that have been helpful to me and invite you to sift through them for anything that might be useful to you.

1. AN OPEN DOORWAY FOR JESUS

My stubborn nature is just beginning to understand and accept that I must always leave an open doorway in my thinking to allow right ideas to come in and replace wrong ones. Throughout my life I have been a person who, despite being personally disorganised, likes complete sets of things. On what most people would consider a fairly trivial level, for instance, I turn straight to the set meals in the back of the menu when I am in a Chinese restaurant, thus causing considerable annoyance to my family, who object to their choice of food being controlled by my completion neurosis.

Similarly, but obviously on a different level, our knowledge of the ways of God and appropriate responses to him will never be provided by turning to the back of the Bible and selecting list A, B, C, or D. There is a lifetime of discovery to be undertaken, and the adventure will be terribly truncated and unsatisfactory if I am not ready and, as far as being a member of the human species will allow me, willing to be wrong. When it comes to the crunch, will I freely place my stock of cherished certainties like sad, surrendered weapons at the injured feet of Jesus? I hope I have done that once or twice in the past. I hope I will be able to do it in the future.

PETER AND THE GENTILE

In this connection I have always found it helpful and inspiring to remember what happened to Simon Peter in Joppa, as recorded in the tenth chapter of Acts.

> About noon the next day, as they were on their journey and approaching the city, Peter went up on the roof to pray. He became hungry and wanted something to eat; and while it was being prepared, he fell into a trance. He saw the heaven open and something like a large sheet coming down, being lowered to the ground by its four corners. In it were all kinds of four-footed creatures and reptiles and birds of the air. Then he heard a voice saying, "Get up, Peter; kill and eat." But Peter said, "By no means, Lord; for I have never eaten anything that is profane or unclean." The voice said to him again, a second time, "What God has made clean, you must not call profane." This happened three times, and the thing was suddenly taken up to heaven. (10:9–16 NRSV)

Make no mistake about it, this vivid dream picture would have been an absolute nightmare for a man who remained a Jew by habit and training regardless of his spiritual awakening by Jesus. The very idea of eating such foul creatures! Reptiles! Disgusting! In fact, of course, God had sent this graphic vision to prepare Peter for the arrival of the servants of Cornelius, a devout centurion who had been instructed by an angel to send for Peter. The idea of having dealings with a Gentile must have been almost on a par with the thought of eating snakes, but it is apparent that Peter was equipped with that essential doorway in his thinking that I mentioned previously.

His readiness to substitute a right idea for a wrong one is clearly evidenced in this speech, found later in the same chapter, a speech made after he entered the house of Cornelius on the following day to find a large gathering of the centurion's relatives and friends waiting for him.

And as he talked with him, he went in and found that many
had assembled; and he said to them, "You yourselves know that
it is unlawful for a Jew to associate with or to visit a Gentile;
but God has shown me that I should not call anyone profane or
unclean. So when I was sent for, I came without objection. Now
may I ask why you sent for me?" (10:27–29 NRSV)

As I am sure you know, Peter's visit resulted in conversion
and baptism in water and the Spirit for Cornelius and many
of his friends and relatives. News of this event subsequently
put Peter under pressure to explain his "bizarre" actions to
the highly critical body of believers in Jerusalem. They must
have been doing pretty well doorway-wise as well, judging
by their response to Peter's words, recorded in the eleventh
chapter of Acts.

When they heard this, they were silenced. And they praised
God, saying, "Then God has given even to the Gentiles the
repentance that leads to life." (11:18 NRSV)

Giant whatnots from tiny thingamabobs grow, don't
they? Thank goodness Peter was obedient to the meaning of
the vision. Mind you, associating with Gentiles might have
been an overwhelming relief after the horror of suspecting
that God could be asking him to actually snack on lizards
and frogs.

I feel quite sure that most of you are familiar with Dr
Luke's account of the conversion of Cornelius, either vaguely
or in detail. If you are not, do read it from beginning to end.
Like many episodes in Acts, it really is a very good story. But
it is more than that. What can we make the lesson of this
story of Peter's obedience do for us and our understanding of
the need for God to be authentic in our lives? A little or a lot,
I guess. I have an idea. Feeling brave? I am not sure if I am.
Let us consider the following.

DOGMATIC ABOUT JESUS

One of the burning issues in the worldwide church at present is that of Christianity and homosexuality. Whatever your point of view, you must be unified in your agreement with me so far, surely. Right. Hackles rising? Predictable. Control those hackles.

As we all know, there is one whole section of the Christian church that is in no doubt at all that homosexual practices are forbidden by Scripture and cannot be condoned under any circumstances. It is not a question of debate and opinion, because we are passionately committed to obedience, and God has stated his view quite clearly.

We are also fully aware of another, equally vocal and impassioned faction whose members believe that God does not distinguish between opposite and same-sex relationships, because, for him, the only important criteria are love and commitment. The Bible may appear to frown on gay relationships, this group will say, but it does preach love and loyalty as priorities, and in any case there are plenty of other biblical injunctions that most of us seem to have abandoned – women covering their hair in church, to name but one. Why does this one have to be any different?

One question: Do you belong to either of these groups? Another question: Do you have a doorway in your thinking that is open to new truth about the will and the person of God? These two questions are not mutually exclusive, and that is my main point.

Let us suppose that you are among those who do not condone homosexual behaviour. Here is my question. Please do your best not to duck it. If Jesus unequivocally revealed to you that for one divinely approved reason or another, it is within his will that same-sex relationships should be welcomed in the church, would you abandon your present perspective and be thankful that the truth has prevailed? Or would you continue to argue that Scripture supports your view and that God himself is wrong?

Perhaps you are one of those who sees no reason to criticise homosexual practice. Here is the same question. Please do your best not to duck it. Your opponents didn't. If Jesus clearly indicated to you that for sound spiritual and biblical reasons, the church must not teach or accept that homosexual activity is approved by God, would you thank him for his correction of your viewpoint and announce your change of attitude to others, or would you continue to argue that the logic of love shows this to be a cruel nonsense?

Try not to be distracted by the specific example that I have chosen. If you allow that to happen, you have let the real issue pass you by. Choose another example if you want. The real issue is not, in the context of this argument anyway, whether homosexual behaviour is acceptable or not, but that if our top priority truly is Jesus, there will be only one absolutely nonprovisional dogma, and that will be the need to establish a loving and obedient relationship with him. It has only been possible for the tolerance of slavery, poverty, apartheid, and the doctrine of salvation through works to be perceived as false and to be overthrown during the last two thousand years because of the hard work and courage of Christians who maintained an open door into their hearts for startlingly unfamiliar and unfashionable truths.

But the other side of that coin is just as crucial. We must never forget that the purity of the gospel has been preserved by equally courageous believers who have been ready to die before they would allow the clear stream of doctrine to be muddied by heresy. I thank God for all of those resolute people, and I pray with all my heart that you and I will be as brave and obedient as Peter, if and when we are called upon to accept a revelation of truth that seems to be at war with our previous understanding.

To summarise this first point, then: a commitment to authentic Christianity demands a flexibility of attitude and understanding that will allow our perceptions of Jesus and the one true God to change and develop and grow as the Holy Spirit teaches and works in us. We are not talking about accepting heresies. Indeed, we may be talking about recanting one or two. Do not preach your pet idol. Open a door. Guard that door carefully, of course, and be as wary as you like, but keep the hinges oiled. Something may be coming through.

2. A SULKY PROPHET

What else will help us in our search to understand the true nature of God? The obvious answer is, of course, studying the Bible, and primarily looking at the Son of God himself. Before we do the latter, though, let us look at an Old Testament character, one who was mentioned quite significantly by Jesus in the course of his teaching. This man's story has much to say about the fundamental character of God and the kind of relationship that you and I might dare to have with him. The name of the man is Jonah, and I cannot help wishing that he could be sitting here in my study now. I may be wrong, but I suspect that he and I would get on rather well.

I gather that for a very long time, critical scholars doubted the historical nature of the book of Jonah, preferring to see it as a typical Jewish folktale, an allegory or myth written with a view to teaching abstract truth about God. In more recent years, however, it seems that excavations have shown the city or district of Nineveh to be very close in size to the measurements given by the writer of this book. Elements of the story also agree with what we know about the situation in Nineveh at this time. So there we are. Who knows? What we can be sure of is that God wants it in the Bible and that it makes a fascinating and enlightening tale, beginning with the prophet's dramatic attempt to escape from the burden of a task that held no appeal for him at all.

> Now the word of the Lord came to Jonah son of Amittai, saying, "Go at once to Nineveh, that great city, and cry out against it; for their wickedness has come up before me." But Jonah set out to flee to Tarshish from the presence of the Lord. He went down to Joppa and found a ship going to Tarshish; so he paid his fare and went on board, to go with them to Tarshish, away from the presence of the Lord.
>
> But the Lord hurled a great wind upon the sea, and such a mighty storm came upon the sea that the ship threatened to break up. Then the mariners were afraid, and each cried to his god. They threw the cargo that was in the ship into the sea, to lighten it for them. Jonah, meanwhile, had gone down into the hold of the ship and had lain down, and was fast asleep. The captain came and said to him, "What are you doing sound asleep? Get up, call on your god! Perhaps the god will spare us a thought so that we do not perish." (1:1–6 NRSV)

After casting lots, the terrified sailors find that the lot falls upon Jonah, and they become very agitated indeed when they learn that he is on the run from the presence of the Lord. What should they do? Jonah knows. He has no doubt about what they should do. Chuck me overboard, he tells them, and your troubles will be at an end. Caught between an angry God and the deep blue sea, the crew of the ship do their energetic best to avoid this drastic final solution, but frantic rowing doesn't help, and at last no choice is left to them. Over the wildly swaying side of the boat into the boiling sea goes one disobedient prophet, and immediately the storm ceases to rage.

The next part of the story may well qualify as the most widely known event in the entire Bible, certainly as far as generations of Sunday school children are concerned. Jonah is swallowed by a great fish (not a whale, according to the boring experts – I hope they never solemnly inform us that Daniel's lions were actually meerkats), and after three days and nights he is spewed up onto dry land, all ready to go and get on with the job he was supposed to do in the first place. And one has to say that despite his earlier reluctance, he does it well. He must have. In the course of a day's walk towards the centre of the city, he puts the fear of God into the locals. Literally. In fact, so well does he do his job that the king of Nineveh leads the entire populace into an act of repentance, and as a result God changes his mind and decides not to bring calamity to the city after all.

Once a prophet, always a prophet. That was Jonah's blessing or curse, depending on how you look at it. Once he was actually on the job, there was no way he could have toned down the message. He must have always known that about himself, just as he knew enough about God to strongly suspect that the citizens of Nineveh would be forgiven if they really knuckled down and repented. Jonah was very cross.

> But this was very displeasing to Jonah, and he became angry. He prayed to the Lord and said, "O Lord! Is not this what I said while I was still in my own country? That is why I fled to Tarshish at the beginning; for I knew that you are a gracious God and merciful, slow to anger, and abounding in steadfast love, and ready to relent from punishing. And now, O Lord, please take my life from me, for it is better for me to die than to live." (4:1 – 3)

This is a very unusual and slightly confusing little speech, don't you think? Generally, when person A is angry with person B, she or he hurls insults at him or her, usually the most hurtful things they can think of at the time. I cannot help thinking that I might be very pleased if, in the process of losing their temper with me, someone furiously accused me of being gracious, merciful, slow to anger, abounding in steadfast love, and ready to relent from punishing. Chance would be a fine thing!

I suppose the point is that Jonah felt quite safe in sounding off at God precisely because he knew these qualities of love and restraint would be extended to him just as they had been extended to the people of Nineveh. I am reminded of my youngest son who, as a very small boy, countered a very stern speech from me with the following confident assertion from halfway up the stairs: "Anyway, you love me, so you'll be nice to me in a minute!" Absolutely right, of course, and I was too amused and disconcerted to continue my crossness with any real force or authenticity.

I doubt if God was disconcerted by Jonah's burst of bad temper, but he may have been a little amused, and he obviously decided that it was time to teach his sulky prophet a lesson. He caused a bush or tree to grow up in the place where Jonah was sitting gloomily, waiting to see what would happen (or rather, not happen) to the city. The shade provided by the bush was very agreeable, but by morning a worm, obviously a creature that was on the divine payroll, had eaten away the root of the new growth so that the tree withered.

As the temperature rose to unbearable heights, a sultry wind came up from the east, and Jonah was so overwhelmed by the heat of the sun that he became faint and announced to God once again that he would rather die than live. It is at this point, in the final paragraph of the book, that God spells out the lesson he wants Jonah to learn.

> But God said to Jonah, "Is it right for you to be angry about the bush?" And he said, "Yes, angry enough to die." Then

the Lord said, "You are concerned about the bush, for which you did not labour and which you did not grow; it came into being in a night and perished in a night. And should I not be concerned about Nineveh, that great city, in which there are more than a hundred and twenty thousand people who do not know their right hand from their left, and also many animals?" (4:9–11 NRSV)

What can we learn about the nature of God from the book of Jonah? Four things stand out.

TRUE OBEDIENCE

First of all, it is clear that obedience comes very high on the divine list of priorities. Jonah was given a job to do, and everything else was put on hold until, covered in whale goo, he was ready to squelch off and shout at Nineveh. Having negotiated one or two loops of my own to get back to the place where I am supposed to be, I sympathise with the prophet, but I also recognise that it really does make sense to do what you are told at the time when you receive your orders. Having said that, it is interesting to note what happened after Jonah spilled the beans to the sailors and they had thrown him overboard. The calming of the storm had a very powerful effect on those fellows:

> Then the men feared the Lord even more, and they offered a sacrifice to the Lord and made vows. (1:16)

In other words, as soon as Jonah embarked on the curve in the loop that would take him back to obedience, God was able to use the situation to draw people to him. In one important sense it seems that God is not proud. He will use me, you, and anyone else who has turned their faltering steps back onto the right road as a channel to bring Jesus to those we meet on the way.

God does not hold grudges. We think we know that. But do we believe it as well as knowing it? If, like so many of us, you have done a Jonah and you now want to get back into the will of God, bear this in mind. It will be business as usual almost before you have time to take a breath, and the past will be just a bad dream. How good that will feel.

TRUE CREATIVITY

Second, I can see in the vivid adventures of Jonah the creativity and ingenuity with which God prefers to operate in the lives of individuals. What an extraordinary succession of events! Let me tell you something that puzzles and depresses me when I chew it over too much. Despite the Bible being stuffed to the gunnels with evidence of God's detailed, individual planning in the lives of each of his followers, we still hear preachers and teachers droning on about the business of following Jesus as though it were some item of regulation-issue spiritual machinery that has to be mastered properly before it can be used in the prescribed and identical way.

Of course there are broad principles involved in our dealings with God, and for much of the time we are not allowed to see exactly what he is doing or planning, but there are certain things I know for sure because I have had four children myself. I love them very much, and I think they love me. I have tried to love them all consistently, but, especially when they were little, it would have been madness to apply some unvarying, formulaic parental response to the ways in which their individual differences were expressed. Apart from anything else, life would have been much less rich and interesting for all of us. God must be just a tad wiser than me, don't you think?

It is up to us. We can treat our faith as though it is the equivalent of spending the rest of our lives learning to pick out "Twinkle, Twinkle Little Star" badly on one string of an out-of-tune, cracked guitar, or we can ask God to let us lose ourselves in the completed symphony of his will for us and resolve to follow that music whenever we are allowed to hear it and to wherever it takes us. Which shall we choose? Which shall I choose? Today, feeling quite fired up, I want to choose the latter course. I hope I shall feel the same tomorrow.

TRUE SAFETY

The third lesson that I learn about God from the book of Jonah is that he will always keep us safe, but that is an ambiguous little four-letter word, and I want to be very clear about what I mean by it. It strikes me as interesting and significant that the writer of this account has Jonah sending up a prayer of praise and thanksgiving from the belly of the fish. Thanksgiving for what? Praise about what? He has just been thrown over the side of a ship, and now he is lying in the damp, squishy darkness, gripped by the most appalling piscatorial nightmare it is possible to imagine, a ghastly happening that makes *Jaws* look like a picnic on the riverbank. What does the prophet say?

> I called to the Lord out of my distress, and he answered me; out of the belly of Sheol I cried, and you heard my voice. (2:2 NRSV)

Then, a little later:

> As my life was ebbing away, I remembered the Lord; and my prayer came to you, into your holy temple. Those who worship vain idols forsake their true loyalty. But I with the voice of thanksgiving will sacrifice to you; what I have vowed I will pay. Deliverance belongs to the Lord! (2:7–9 NRSV)

Deliverance? Is the man completely mad? No, I don't think so. I think he is celebrating the fact that he is safe in the most accurate sense of the word. God clearly wanted Jonah to get this task accomplished, so he gave him a second chance. Many of us are familiar with the second, third, fourth, fifth, and more chances that God gives us. He could have given up on Jonah after he ran away to Tarshish and got them to send some less stroppy character along from the minor-prophet agency. But he didn't.

No, although none of us is indispensable to the work of God, each of us will be suited to different tasks because of who we are and how we operate. Jonah was the man for the job. But it wasn't just that, was it? God wanted Jonah to be safe, as he wants all his children to be safe, and the way to do that was to make sure he ended up in the centre of his Master's will. I think we can reasonably assume that to be true for us as well.

I have said a lot more on this subject in the first part of this book, so I won't go on and on about it here. Suffice it to say that followers of Jesus can be genuinely safe in an armchair in front of the fire, or in an underground prison while undergoing torture, or as they are being stoned to death, or in a fiery furnace, or in the discovery that they have breast cancer at the very point when they are due for a rest after years of caring for handicapped children, or in a catastrophic staff meeting, or in a shipwreck, or in the midst of grief, or in hunger, or in a supermarket, or in pain, or in the course of a good meal with friends, or in the belly of a big fish, or in a nice hot bath with Mozart playing in the next room, or in a palace, or in the most depressing house on the most depressing street in the most run-down inner-city slum, as long as they are where they are supposed to be.

Forgive me for bludgeoning you around the head with my point, but something tells me that we in the Western church are so entrenched in a quite different, much more material view of safety that we need to be dragged kicking and screaming over the parapet and into that war-torn place of spiritual reality where we will acknowledge and try to live in the truth of this indisputable fact.

TRUE COMPASSION

My fourth Jonah-inspired lesson is, for me and for this section of my book, the most important one of all. How can I best express it? If God were a computer programme, he would default to tender compassion. Jonah knew it. That was why he tried to run away to Tarshish in the first place. It must have happened several times before. The same pattern repeating itself. God sends out the order to his servant, Jonah piles into some sinful community with awesome and effective warnings of imminent punishment, the sinful community repents in sackcloth and ashes, God is delighted and forgives them all, and Jonah is left wishing that he could disappear into a big hole in the ground, instead of having to feebly explain that, well, yes, God does sometimes forgive sinners even though he has previously threatened, through Jonah the sulky minor prophet, to wipe them and their cattle from the face of the earth.

God loves people. God loves the world. God so loved the world that he entered it in human form to make it possible for as many as possible to live safely with him forever. Please don't ask me to explain exactly what that means or how the implied, mind-boggling logical knots can be untied by mere human brains. But you are very welcome to ask me if I agree with Jonah about the compassion of God, and I will reply, "Yes, yes, yes! I do agree that everything I read and hear and experience in connection with the God who made this world affirms that he has only ever wanted, only ever wants, will only ever want to be at peace with his children, and that whenever or wherever the tiniest of spiritual loopholes makes that possible, he will use it with the powerful and unfathomable passion of a Father who weeps over every lost soul and rejoices with the whole of heaven over each one who is saved. I quite often lose touch with the splendour of that fact, but I do have my own defaulting mechanism, and it invariably takes me back to the Father who waits with a robe, a ring, a fatted calf, and his own open arms for anyone who cares to turn away from the pigs and head for home.

Some people react rather oddly when I talk enthusiastically about the tenderness and compassion of God. Their response reminds me of those television programmes where members of the public bring their antiques along so that experts can value them. You know the programmes I mean. The ones where quite ordinary objects can turn out to be worth an enormous amount of money, or there might be palpable disappointment when great-grandfather's fob watch is revealed to be a cheap reproduction instead of a valuable heirloom. It all adds to the interest and pleasure of the viewing audience. I have noticed a distinct reaction in a certain type of person when they hear the news that an item is worth much more than they had anticipated. Usually a man in his mid to late years, this person receives what anyone else would regard as very good news indeed with a worried frown, pursed lips, and a troubled shake of the head.

"Oh dear!" he seems to be saying to himself. "It's worth a lot of money. Oh dear, oh dear, oh dear! That means I'll have to insure it and wrap it up and put it at the back of a deep, dark cupboard where it can't be stolen, and never look at it again except for when I get it out every five years to renew the insurance and worry about it being so valuable. Oh, dear, I wish I'd never come ..."

As I said, this is a rough approximation to the manner in which some folk respond when I wax lyrical about the compassion of God. It seems to worry them. The light goes out of their eyes. They chew their lower lip. They are quick to remind me that as well as being compassionate, God is awesome and just and hates all sin. One gets the impression that they would rather wrap up the compassion and put it into a deep, dark cupboard where it can continue to be valuable but not upset or trouble anyone by actually being visible. Is it a matter of confidence? Do we find it very difficult to accept that in God we really do find the essence of love? Why on earth would anyone prefer to believe that the thunderbolt-flinging side of God is his true nature, and the kind, fatherly side no more than the result of infrequent lapses into uncharacteristic weakness?

Jonah was not the only Old Testament character who understood the compassion of God. Root out your concordance or borrow one from someone else and take a look. Here, for example, are some verses from the wonderful Psalm 103:

> The Lord is merciful and gracious, slow to anger and abounding in steadfast love.
> He will not always accuse, nor will he keep his anger forever.
> He does not deal with us according to our sins, nor repay us according to our iniquities.
> For as the heavens are high above the earth, so great is his steadfast love toward those who fear him;
> as far as the east is from the west, so far he removes our transgressions from us.
> As a father has compassion for his children, so the Lord has compassion for those who fear him.
> For he knows how we are made; he remembers that we are dust. (vv. 8–14 NRSV)

I feel quite sure that there are many more lessons to be learned about the nature of God from the fascinating story of Jonah, but these four have been the ones that have caught my eye on reading it through this time. To summarise:

- Obedience is very high on God's list, and there is little point in trying to escape, either by ship or by retreating into our own minds or by any other means.
- God exercises great ingenuity and creativity in organising and shaping the lives of believers.
- He will keep us safe, not as the world keeps us safe, but by bringing us to the centre of his will.
- It is the fundamental nature of God to be compassionate. His forgiveness is always more than ready to meet our repentance.

What can I say about Jonah in conclusion? Well, two or three years ago, Bridget and I went to see a movie called *Bruce Almighty*. Starring wild-eyed Jim Carrey and the supremely talented Morgan Freeman, this film tells the story of a human being who, for the usual totally unbelievable but essential plot-driving reasons, is allowed to be God for a short time, or rather to have God's miraculous powers at his disposal. The film is entertaining enough in itself, but I was especially taken with Morgan Freeman's portrayal of God. Freeman's God is a wholly confident but laid-back character with smiling eyes and an aura of intense, restrained joy. He laughs delightedly at Bruce's jokes, but apart from allowing him enough rope to tie himself into hopeless knots, he refuses to allow him to get away with anything.

This is a close approximation to the God that I perceive when I read the story of Jonah, and it is also very much in line with the firm, interesting, kindly, caring Father who has been revealed to my gradually opening eyes in the years since I first said yes to Jesus nearly forty years ago.

3. THE IMAGE OF THE INVISIBLE GOD

So in our exploration of ways to ensure that we avoid the idol-worship trap and discover the true nature of God, we have talked about the need to leave a door open in our spiritual understanding, and we have learned a little more about the Creator from his relationship with sulky old Jonah. Now we turn to the most accurate source of information that is available to us. We turn to Jesus.

What is our authority for regarding Jesus as the primary source of information about God? Let me suggest one answer to that question. It comes from the first chapter of Colossians, and if, by the way, you think I sound like a Jesus nut in this book, just take a look at what Paul has to say about his Master.

> He is the image of the invisible God, the firstborn of all creation; for in him all things in heaven and on earth were created, things visible and invisible, whether thrones or dominions or rulers or powers – all things have been created through him and for him. He himself is before all things, and in him all things hold together. He is the head of the body, the church; he is the beginning, the firstborn from the dead, so that he might come to have first place in everything. For in him all the fullness of God was pleased to dwell, and through him God was pleased to reconcile to himself all things, whether on earth or in heaven, by making peace through the blood of his cross. (1:15–20 NRSV)

In the first few words of this passage, Paul is saying that when we look at Jesus, we are able to see a clear picture of God – very interesting when I consider the firstborn sons or daughters of people I know. I see it in my own life and, most graphically, in the mirror that hangs in our hall a few feet away from me as I write. Whether I wish to own or distance myself from the person my father was, I cannot deny that he is visible in me. How much more must this be the case with the Son of God?

Let us look at one dominant aspect of the nature of Jesus, as revealed in the gospels, and discover how it informs us about the nature of the Father. Jonah has already taught us this lesson, but we might as well confirm it through the gospels. Jesus was and is filled with compassion for those in need, just as his Father is, and just as we should be if we really do want to be like him.

I was given a head start when it comes to understanding about compassion for others. My mother, who did quite a good job of reflecting God herself, was one of the most naturally caring people I have known. I shall never match the practical generosity that characterised her faith. She had very little money, but that certainly did not stop her from giving incessantly, sharing her time, energy, and resources with anyone who was in need.

For instance, every night for years my mother would go round to the house next door at about half past nine to help her elderly neighbour up the stairs to bed. My mother's knees were very weak and painful, and Elsie Jones was hardly able to walk at all. Because of this, the only way that the task could be accomplished was for mum to sit on the stairs with her head wedged under Elsie's bottom, pushing the old lady up step by step with frequent stops for the two of them to get their breath. Very far from being the visual epic it might have been, but I am prepared to wager that the hosts of heaven greeted this nightly exercise with more applause than those spectacles that might appear much grander and greater to the human eye.

My mother has gone to join her neighbour in heaven now, and both of them now have new, highly efficient legs. I imagine mum must have been astonished to discover how much she and Jesus have in common, not least this gift of responding to the problems and needs of suffering human beings.

All that my mother did and was arose from the life of Jesus in her, the same Jesus who, two thousand years ago, responded with compassion and healing to so many troubled people, even on those rare days when he had been looking forward to a little time off. I love to read the following passage from Mark's gospel.

> From there he set out and went away to the region of Tyre. He entered a house and did not want anyone to know he was there. Yet he could not escape notice, but a woman whose little daughter had an unclean spirit immediately heard about him, and she came and bowed down at his feet. Now the woman was a Gentile, of Syrophoenician origin. She begged him to cast the demon out of her daughter. He said to her, "Let the children be fed first, for it is not fair to take the children's food and throw it to the dogs." But she answered him, "Sir, even the dogs under the table eat the children's crumbs." Then he said to her, "For saying that, you may go – the demon has left your daughter." So she went home, found the child lying on the bed, and the demon gone. (7:24 – 30 NRSV)

She got it dead right, didn't she? The combination of wit and need was irresistible to him. She got what she wanted, of course. So did the quartet of ingenious chaps who devised a novel way of bringing their crippled friend to the Great Healer's immediate notice.

> When he returned to Capernaum after some days, it was reported that he was at home. So many gathered around that there was no longer room for them, not even in front of the door; and he was speaking the word to them. Then some people came, bringing to him a paralysed man, carried by four of them. And when they could not bring him to Jesus because of the crowd, they removed the roof above him; and

after having dug through it, they let down the mat on which the paralytic lay. When Jesus saw their faith, he said to the paralytic, "Son, your sins are forgiven." Now some of the scribes were sitting there, questioning in their hearts, "Why does this fellow speak in this way? It is blasphemy! Who can forgive sins but God alone?" At once Jesus perceived in his spirit that they were discussing these questions among themselves; and he said to them, "Why do you raise such questions in your hearts? Which is easier, to say to the paralytic, 'Your sins are forgiven,' or to say, 'Stand up and take your mat and walk'? But so that you may know that the Son of Man has authority on earth to forgive sins"—he said to the paralytic—"I say to you, stand up, take your mat and go to your home." And he stood up, and immediately took the mat and went out before all of them; so that they were all amazed and glorified God, saying, "We have never seen anything like this!" (Mark 2:1–12 NRSV)

No doubt the onlookers were amazed, and it is no wonder that they glorified God. Just imagine, though, the rollicking joy with which those five men must have pushed their way out past the waiting crowds in that packed house, their memories forever and ever alight with the laughter and approval that they had seen in the Master's face as he rewarded their faith and their drive and their concern for a friend with forgiveness and healing.

Jesus responded to passion and need. One day when we are in heaven, we shall meet people who will witness freely to that fact. The centurion with the sick servant who so ably demonstrated his understanding of the way in which authority works will tell us how Jesus granted his wish on the spot, having been amazed by the passion and certainty of a Gentile's faith. Bartimaeus, the blind man who refused to be silenced by the crowd, will fill us in on how the Master heard his voice above all others, felt the depth of his need, and restored his sight. Clamouring to add his tale to the others, we shall hear from the father of the sick boy whom the disciples were unable to help, the man who so passionately and succinctly expressed the fact that he did believe but needed help with his unbelief.

The queue will be a very long one, but here is another of my favourites. You will find it recorded in the seventh chapter of Luke's gospel:

> Soon afterward, Jesus went to a town called Nain, and his disciples and a large crowd went along with him. As he approached the town gate, a dead person was being carried out – the only son of his mother, and she was a widow. And a large crowd from the town was with her. When the Lord saw her, his heart went out to her and he said, "Don't cry."
>
> Then he went up and touched the coffin, and those carrying it stood still. He said, "Young man, I say to you, get up!" The dead man sat up and began to talk, and Jesus gave him back to his mother.
>
> They were all filled with awe and praised God. "A great prophet has appeared among us," they said. "God has come to help his people!" This news about Jesus spread throughout Judea and the surrounding country. (7:11–17)

On seeing this weeping mother, did Jesus have a sudden vision of his own mother after the crucifixion, bereft of her son and weeping for the blessed ordinariness of a distant past that could never return? I don't know. I hope I shall be able to ask him one day, perhaps in some quiet moment when he and I and others are flying peacefully across the universe checking progress on the construction of the new earth from a good vantage point.

This is such a sweet story. And very significantly for our understanding of evangelism, it does not begin with a desire to make converts or to change people's attitudes. The incident, and hence the effects that spring from it, begins with a moment of truly spontaneous sympathy and compassion. I am overwhelmed by the thought of the heart of Jesus going out so simply and generously to this humble daughter of Adam who has lost her only son and can see only darkness in the life that awaits her. He just wanted to make everything all right for her, and he was able to tell her to stop crying with confidence because power and compassion were intertwined in him.

And I am more and more convinced that this should be the way for us as well. We should be feeling and sorrowing and responding and letting our hearts go out to whoever needs them, relying on the power of the Holy Spirit who lives and loves through us to do all the healing and life-changing things that need to follow from these spontaneous acts of reaching out.

I say all this as if I really do know what I am talking about. Well, I can assure you I genuinely want to behave in this way. I yearn to be as spontaneously appreciative as Jesus was and is of profound need in others. My prayer is for more of the right kind of confidence, the kind that children sometimes have, the kind of confidence I remember having, many years ago, in the kindness of my mother.

I must have been about eight years old. A friend and I were playing in the playground just down the road from my home. My friend tried to do something very clever on one of the swings and fell off, cutting his knee quite badly. He lay on the ground crying and clutching his knee as it bled. I quivered with eight-year-old sympathy and uncertainty. Then the obvious solution occurred to me.

"Let's go round to my house," I said. "My mum'll wash it and put a bandage on."

We limped home on three legs, and she did do those things when we got there. She gave my friend a glass of lemonade in addition to looking after his knee. Of course she did. I knew she would. I knew her, you see. Not for one moment did I fear that my confidence was misplaced. I knew I could rely on her to live up to the promise I had made to my injured friend. The valuable pattern of that relationship of trust is still within me, and there have been some occasions in adult life when it has been closely replicated in my dealings with those who are in need of compassion. Secretly or openly I pass them on to Jesus to have their knees washed and bandaged and to be comforted and reassured. I wish I did it more. I wish we all would do it more.

I have no idea if you or I will ever be entrusted with the task of miraculously feeding 5,000 people who have forgotten to bring any lunch with them. Calming storms and raising the dead to life might seem a little beyond us. Changing water into wine would be a fantastically popular party trick, but I don't know if God will ever call on us to perform it. What I do know for sure is that Jesus is still tenderly reaching out to those who have a need, still having his heart wrenched by the sight of crowds that are like sheep without a shepherd. There is work to be done. It might involve miracles. It will certainly involve hard work. There will be pain, because the pain of the Lord Jesus will pierce our hearts.

Our God is many things, but the book of Jonah and the life of Jesus suggest that the core of his being and the motive for his involvement with us is love. We need to leave open a door in our perception to continually admit and refresh our realisation that he defaults to compassion, reaching out to those in need from a heart that is filled with care. It is true that there are many other things to learn about the Creator of the universe. We know that indignation, justice, and anger are important aspects of our God. Learn about them by all means. Teach them and preach them and debate them and warn people about some of them. But if we have failed to comprehend the centrality of love and tenderness in the nature of our heavenly Father, then we do not understand him at all, and the God we represent to other people will be a false one.

My Encounters
with the Tender Jesus

ANOTHER PLACE

I am sitting in my living room at home. I have put a compact disc in the sound system, and now I am flopped in a chair waiting for the music to begin. There is no one else in the house at the moment, which is just as well, because I am feeling frazzled and irritable about everything. This is one of those mornings when life seems to be heaping itself on top of my head like a flumpingly heavy pile of those smelly, scratchy old cream-coloured blankets that you don't see any more, robbing me of fresh air and the clear light of day and squashing everything out of perspective.

Not for the first time, I am seething with annoyance at God for being perfect. I would like to give him a piece of my mind, but – I ask you – what on earth is the point in complaining about and finding fault with someone who never actually does anything wrong? Omnipotence and omniscience must be pretty useful shields. What are we pathetic human beings expected to do when all of our little dark darts of negative feeling get deflected by the power of pure light and come flying back to stick themselves in us?

I tell myself that if one of our cats was around at the moment, I might kick it, but I know I wouldn't really. Why not? Well, because I'm supposed to be a Christian, and people who are supposed to be Christians don't lunge out at cats just to relieve their own frustrations. That's the theory anyway. Stupid theory! Doesn't appeal to me in the slightest today. The way I'm feeling at the moment, I think I'd be able to talk myself into kicking any living thing that was foolish enough to cross my path. Beetles, crocodiles, canaries, any old living thing.

A bit washed out altogether, I suppose. That's the main thing that's wrong with me. That, and being me. Just being my boringly inescapable self. A general weariness about the endlessly repeated process of discovering how fundamentally useless I am. Yes, I know that's a good thing in a way, and on my better days I would be happily talking or writing away about how that realisation can create space for the Holy Spirit to work through us.

Not today though. Not today. Today I don't care what it creates. I couldn't care less. And I don't care what the Holy Spirit does or doesn't do. I've had enough of the whole miserable, grinding business. I wish I was sitting under a parasol on a beach in the Caribbean, sipping cocktails and reading mindless literature before going back to my five-star hotel for a seafood banquet and a night of dreamless sleep, untainted by constant thoughts of how we might be able to gather enough twiddly religious nuts and bolts to somehow hold the whole unwieldy thing together yet again.

The music I am about to listen to is one of my favourite albums. *The Journey*, a collection of instrumental tracks, was written and recorded some years ago by a duo called Simeon and John. Both happen to be Christians, and both are skilled and versatile musicians. In this collection John majors on the classical guitar, while Simeon plays a variety of wind instruments, including the panpipes, his speciality. There is intimacy and passion in their music, a useful combination for those whose souls are in need of soothing.

I doubt if it will manage to be soothing enough on this occasion. If you were unfortunate enough to be here, you would almost be able to see the spikes sticking out of me. Imagine it – spikes and smelly old blankets. It won't be easy for anything or anyone to get past that lot.

The CD begins to play.

The first piece leaves me stubbornly unmoved, but there is something about the plaintive guitar solo at the opening of the next track that manages to slip under my defences and nudge me into an unexpected train of thought. For some reason I find myself remembering my beautiful seventeen-year-old daughter Kate when she was a little girl. In my mind's eye I see her on the one or two occasions when she became awkward and difficult in the early evening. These memories are especially vivid because they were so exceptional. Kate was a consistently serene and sunny child. I recall how puzzled and troubled I was when I first witnessed this different kind of behaviour. What had got into my friendly little daughter to make her so unexpectedly loud and argumentative? And how should I respond? I had already had three sons, but parenting never seemed to get much easier. Should I become stern and be a little bit cross, or was it better just to wait until the phase passed?

My questions were answered when Kate turned her small figure towards me as if she had made a sudden, unavoidable decision, and flung out her arms in a wide and heartbreakingly vulnerable gesture. As she spoke, her mouth crumpled at the corners in defeat, and her eyes filled with tears.

"Daddy, I'm so *tired!*"

Any negative feelings that might have chilled my response melted away instantly. She was nothing but a little bundle of need, and at this moment all she needed was me. Placing my hands under her arms, I swung her up into the air and allowed her bonelessly abandoned body to mould itself against my torso, her two skinny legs, weighted by the sandals on her feet, dangling like a pair of inanimate things somewhere down near my stomach. Her last conscious act of the day was to slot her hot, tear-stained face into the well-worn hollow between my chin and my neck. She was probably fast asleep and dreaming before we reached the top of the stairs.

Dear Kate. Dear girl.

The third track is beginning. This is probably my favourite. It is called "Another Place". The tone is one of ineffable sadness and consolation. It is a sympathetic sound, a warm tide of understanding and encouragement. The music seems to wrap around me like a shawl or like the best and most comfortable kind of blanket. Now I seem to have run out of everything, and my own eyes are filling with tears. There is nothing I can do about it. I have nothing left. I find myself crying out to God in a weak voice, much as Kate used to cry out to me.

"Lord, I can't handle it all at the moment. All the words and the preaching and the trying to get things right, and the questions and the answers and the stuff written in books, and the funny ways of behaving in church, and the wondering what on earth's going on half the time and the rubbish that goes rushing round my head. Lord, I just want to be held and reassured and loved and looked after – only for a little while, and then I'll go back to caring about all those things again, I promise. Thank you for loving me today. Amen."

WHAT DO YOU THINK OF WHAT I DO?

It is 1993. I am within a final point of coming to the end of an address that I am delivering to people gathered at a church in Pretoria, the financial capital of South Africa.

I am at the start of a short but fairly intense speaking tour, and already I have found the country to be at a level of tension that is almost unbearable. Next year the all-important national elections will be held, and no one can be quite sure whether the recently released ANC leader, Nelson Mandela, has the personal and political strength to hold the different elements in the country together. He will need to perform this awesome feat if the escalation of conflict and violence that many have predicted is to be avoided. Some speak of a bloodbath. Yesterday a lady I was sitting with burst into tears in the middle of our conversation on some completely different topic.

"I'm sorry," she said. "It's just terrible at the moment. I'm so very frightened."

She represents hundreds of thousands, perhaps millions, of apprehensive South Africans.

Why am I here? Huh! Good question. I am here because someone asked me to come and help people to laugh in the middle of a very unfunny situation. It is the only sort of request that could have brought me to this place of social, political, and racial turmoil. I have no "word from the Lord" for South Africa. Some South African Christians, like many believers in our own troubled province of Northern Ireland, have told me that they are sick of preachers who fly in from other countries armed with yet another "word" for them.

Besides, my knowledge of the situation here is sketchy and ill informed. I know that one section of this society has cruelly, wickedly oppressed another for years and years. I know also that elements of the church in this country, including, of course, one of my personal heroes, Desmond Tutu, have been able to have a much greater input into the drive towards unity and peace than in many other parts of the world, but that is about all I know. I wish I had read more widely on the subject. I feel so feeble and ignorant. I miss my family.

My talk finishes. I chat with a few people. It seems to have gone all right, whatever that means, but as the last remnants of the crowd move away towards the open doors at the end of the church, a wave of misery passes through me. What was that rubbish I was talking from the front just now? Those thin words. That spurious air of confidence. Why am I not laughing now, after more than an hour of working to bring a smile to the faces of others? This is South Africa, where the problems are immense, and violence waits to fall like poisoned rain from the darkest, most heavily saturated of clouds. I want to go home and be safe and stop pretending I have something to offer.

Everyone has disappeared now. I am the only person left. Even my host at the church and one of the organisers of my tour who is accompanying me have disappeared into a side room to sort something or other out. I don't mind that. I have no wish to share my misery, not with those good people anyway.

I turn towards the east end of the church and look upwards. There, carved in a light-coloured wood that seems to have its own in-built shine, is Jesus on the cross. I look at him. He looks at me. I move a few steps nearer to the carving. The face is very good. Full of pain and sweetness. With my eyes on the carved figure, I speak to Jesus in a very small voice.

"What do you think of what I do?"

There is a pause.

"What do you think of what I do?" replies the sad, sympathetic voice in my mind.

I think of South Africa, of all the terrible things that must have happened here over the last century. The presence of Jesus in the lives of his followers has made a difference, but the whole situation is still ragged and unpredictable. Real progress will take years. Jesus has done the best that is possible, but this beautiful country remains a mess. He would like it to be perfect, but it is not. It breaks his heart.

We weep quietly together in the deserted church, and I stop feeling sorry for myself.

JESUS IN TEARS

It is the mid-nineties, and I am at Spring Harvest, the Christian family festival held at two sites in Great Britain and attended by thousands of believers every year. Audiences at this particular event are always warmly appreciative, and this late-night fringe session has been no exception. As far as I am concerned, it has been one of those hour-long presentations in which I become so relaxed that the order of items I have prepared in advance is no longer relevant. Stories, ideas, poems, and spontaneous asides seem to flow into my mind and out of my mouth with such ease that the conscious effort required is virtually nil. This evening's audience came here to be entertained, and as far as I can tell, they have certainly not been disappointed. There has been a lot of laughter, and the general atmosphere is one of bright togetherness. As the final applause dies and happily chattering queues of people start to drift slowly out of the venue, I am feeling very good about it all.

As I step down from the platform, I notice that a line of smiling people has formed at the side of the stage, presumably waiting to speak to me. Most of them are holding a copy of my latest book, perhaps hoping to ask for a signature. It will be a pleasure. I always enjoy signing books. The thought that someone is actually going to read the words I typed onto my computer screen as I sat alone in my cave of a study so many months ago is still quite surprising to me. My encounter with these people will be another pleasant little interlude, and then I shall go back to my chalet and relax with a film on the television and something to eat and a bottle of wine before going to bed. Mellow. Nice.

Something is wrong. The girl at the front of the queue is not holding one of my books. Nor is she smiling. I know that expression. Her face has been punched by the mindless fist of tragedy. Her whole body is like a container filled to the brim and liable to overflow at the slightest nudge. When I greet her she speaks, and in her voice I can hear the deep vibrations of restrained grief.

"I lost my baby," she says, "only a few days ago. I know nothing can change that, but I just wanted to ask you about–about where Jesus is in that."

I stare at her. The very worst and most useless part of me is annoyed and exasperated that this has happened to spoil an evening that so far has gone so well. And she is at the front of the line, for goodness' sake! When someone comes out with a question like that, you can't spend a few seconds dealing with it and then say, "Next, please!" The prospect of my mellow evening dwindles and fades.

One that is not much better swiftly succeeds the very worst and most useless part of me. This part of me does a quick mental inventory of the types of answers that one usually produces for questions like this. There must be something I can use, surely. Living in the mystery? Greater battle going on elsewhere? Divine context? Power and beauty of suffering? Got to be one of those I can offer her.

Then, thank God, the best part of me, the part that is miraculously inhabited by the Spirit of God, looks into the eyes of this young woman who, at the darkest time in her life, is feeling like a little lost girl, and transfigured by need, she becomes the most important person in the world. For Jesus and for me, she *is* the only queue there ever was, and although there are sometimes special words, I am given none today. There is only one possible answer to her question, only one that I can offer. I hear my own voice breaking slightly as I reply,

"I don't know. I really don't know. I wish I knew. I have not the slightest idea . . . "

She nods. I put my arms around her. It is the clearest message I can offer from the suffering, sympathetic, nail-pierced Christ who, all those years ago, shouted out a question, demanding to know why his God had forsaken him and received no reply from those who were standing by. Love, love, love, out of the reassuring light and into the centre of the lonely dark. She is held as she cries and cries and cries.

THE DEEP, DARK PLACE

I am down in a deep, dark place where the air is bad and there is only the tiniest trace of diffused light. I should explain that I am not a prisoner here. I can leave at any time if I so choose. There is a substantial ladder against the wall that will take me up and out into a world of fresh air and sunlight. Perhaps I will climb that ladder later. Not now, though. Not yet.

I am in the place that is reserved for those who know that they will be forgiven by God but cannot find a way to forgive themselves. I do not want to be exposed to the light, even though it will ultimately heal me. What have I to do with the light or it with me? I cannot believe what I have done, or rather what I have not done.

It began three days ago when a friend named Mark rang me to say that his sister was on the verge of death. Dorothy, a single lady all her life, had been suffering from a painful cancer for almost a year, and now her battle for survival was about to come to an end. I knew quite a lot about Dorothy, having met her several times at Mark's house. I was well aware that Mark, a devout follower of Jesus, had always hoped that these encounters might have resulted in a softening of his sister's militant atheism, but until recently this optimism had appeared to be seriously misplaced. Dorothy was a very likeable, feisty lady, but her attitude to organised religion and Christianity in particular was hard and harsh and loudly expressed, especially to me for some reason. I had sometimes found myself wondering rather dismally if the things I said to her over the years had actually driven her further from faith than might otherwise have been the case.

Then, a few weeks ago, Mark and his sister had turned up at a local meeting where I was speaking. Let me be honest. I found this quite off-putting. Why was Dorothy there? Was she planning to indulge herself with a little pleasurable heckling? I tried not to look in her direction as I spoke, but as many speakers can testify, the face of the person you don't want to look at can have a fatally magnetic attraction. As the evening progressed I was surprised to see that she seemed to be in tears. What was going on? Mark and his sister left too quickly after the meeting for me to catch them and have a chat, but Mark rang me the next day and explained that despite all she had said in the past, Dorothy had recently developed a passionate regard for Jesus. On one level, a purely intellectual one, she still maintained that the whole thing was a nonsense that was not worth bothering with, but on a different level altogether, she was—well, amazingly, she loved him.

Dorothy had wanted to come to the evening meeting where I was due to speak, intent on pursuing the uncomfortable paradox that had pushed its way into her life and perhaps even hoping that she might find a way to resolve it. She had found the meeting very moving, Mark said, although the paradox remained exactly that, and Dorothy was adamant that however she might feel about the Jesus she met in the Bible, nothing was ever going to persuade her to "sign up" and call herself a Christian. I thanked Mark for telling me all this and found myself thinking about Dorothy's unusual inner conflict quite often in the weeks that followed.

Then, three days ago, there was another telephone call. It was Mark. Dorothy was failing fast; in fact, her doctor was not expecting her to survive the week. Mark wanted to know if I could come and talk to Dorothy, perhaps even pray with her to this Jesus whom she loved with her heart if not with her mind.

I said I would. Of course I would. Mark asked when I would go.

I placed the telephone against my chest as I thought through the possibilities. I could have gone the next day, Tuesday. Nothing urgent was planned for that day or for Wednesday. I could have gone. Easily. It would have been no trouble. Either of those days would have been fine.

Lifting the phone once more, I said that I would come on Thursday evening, deliberately giving the impression that the next two days were so heavily booked with crucially important things that it was impossible to do anything before then. Why did I do this? Why did I deliberately put off something so important? I struggled and still struggle to focus on the true answer to this question. There were traces of resentment, left over from those times when Dorothy met anything I had to say about my faith with something close to scorn. There was a fear that I was no solver of paradoxes, a fear of failure in fact, the dread of seeing disappointment and negative confirmation in a dying woman's eyes. Something like that. There may be one or two other dismally trivial things, but I do not care to look at them.

It is Thursday. Mark has just rung me to say that Dorothy died this morning, so there is no need for me to come later on. I mutter some hollow, predictable things before putting down the phone. Sitting by the kitchen table, I stare blankly out of the window. A steel bar of cloud is descending on the Pevensey Levels, promising rain and possibly one of those violent storms that sometimes use this shallow valley as a battlefield.

Dorothy is dead, and I did not go to her. For silly, selfish reasons I neglected to do the thing that might have been exactly what she needed. I have been deliberately disobedient, and now it is too late. There is no Dorothy to visit anymore. I cannot retrieve the situation, and I cannot talk myself into any kind of rationalisation.

Oh, don't get me wrong. Foolish and disobedient I may be, but I am not so vain as to believe that God was depending on me to bring salvation to Dorothy. He has his own way of bridging gaps, and a very soft spot for those who love his Son. No, I think—I pray—that Dorothy is all right, but I am not. I am in this dark cavern of guilt and regret, and there is a subtle but real vanity in my refusal to leave such a place. How can the Creator of the world forgive such sin? How can he even look at me? What value is there in a God who would want this treacherous servant to be part of his kingdom? Groucho Marx said the same thing about not wanting to belong to a club that would have him as a member. In my heart of hearts, I know that this insane way of thinking denies the whole point of the sacrifice made by God in allowing his Son to be so cruelly killed for me. My refusal to make myself vulnerable to his compassion is one more hammer blow to the head of one of those nails that impaled him to the cross.

I am in the dark, and yet, as I said, there is a way out into the light if I choose to take it. I know what will happen if—when—I do. At the top of that ladder over there, I shall be met by Jesus, and in his eyes I shall see the same blend of firmness and compassion with which he looked at the woman taken in adultery 2,000 years ago after everyone else had departed and only the two of them were left.

"Tell me, do you still insist on condemning yourself?" he will ask.

"No," I will reply, taking a deep breath, "I don't think I do."

"Good. In that case, neither do I. Go and sin no more."

I can't stand the dark any more. The decision needs to be made. It will be made. I would like to make it before the storm breaks over this valley. The quality that made Dorothy fall in love with you will draw me back again. I am praying for the courage to put my foot on the first rung of that ladder . . .

CLOSED WOUNDS

It is 2004, and I am sitting on a wooden bench in the Parish Church of King Charles the Martyr in Tunbridge Wells in the county of Kent, just across the other side of Frant Hill from the famous Pantiles Walk. This is one of my favourite buildings in the world. During my very difficult mid-teenage life, this place was one of the refuges that I regularly sought during long hours of meandering aimlessly around the town, penniless and hopeless, yearning for something interesting or constructive to trip me up or divert me from my journey to nowhere.

Times have changed. In those days the church was always unlocked and accessible, and there was rarely anyone else in there on a weekday. That suited me. I found it easier to get on with Nobody than with most other people. It was not just that though, or the fact that it cost nothing to be there, useful as that was on cold or wet days; it was also that the King Charles church was, in itself, such a very beautiful environment. I had read some of the history. Originally built in the seventeenth century, and a permanent structure in the area before the town even existed, it was later worked on by a man with the marvellous name of Henry Doogood, one of Sir Christopher Wren's most famous plasterers. His adornment of the octagonal dome is a pure delight. It delighted me then and it gives me great pleasure now as I sit here revisiting these old memories.

Parallel galleries run along two sides of the church. These were originally used by servants and tradespeople but were also, famously, occupied on a few occasions in the nineteenth century by the sixteen-year-old Princess Victoria, whose visits are commemorated by a large brass plaque on the face of the northern gallery. Down at the front of the church, beside the font, is a notice that I never did tire of reading and reflecting on. It records the story of a travelling gypsy woman who one winter brought in her child from a cruelly hard outside world to be baptised by the minister. Such poverty in the middle of such splendour, I always thought, and such a jewel in the eyes of heaven.

Today I am sitting where I sat so many times in the past, up in the gallery on the south side of the church, looking down over the rows of Victorian pews beneath and across to the place where, all those generations ago, the young girl who was so soon destined to be queen sat and worshiped. I cannot believe that so many years have passed since I first came here.

Suddenly, searingly, a forty-year-old memory surfaces.

It happened here, in this place, when I was sixteen or seventeen. I was sitting up in the balcony, almost in this exact spot, but for once I was not alone. Two other people were with me. One was my very good friend and contemporary, John Hall, who also lived in Tunbridge Wells, and the other was an elderly lady who lived in an old people's home somewhere at the "top", or north end, of Tunbridge Wells. Miss Wilkins spent a fair portion of each of her long days walking the streets and very occasionally expending a small part of her meagre pension on taking tea in one of the innumerable establishments serving the many keen café-dwellers that this town has always attracted.

In the course of my own wanderings I had met this lady, and a friendship had been forged. In our need to fill so many lonely hours, we were rather similar in a way. I learned that Miss Wilkins was a Christian, and somewhat unusually for an older person in those days, she was a believer whose conversation was filled with talk about miracles and spiritual gifts and the immediacy of God.

Nothing in our relationship was arranged or organised. We only ever met by accident. Sometimes I found these encounters exciting and inspiring; at other times the intense and exclusively spiritual nature of our conversations was a little overwhelming. Nevertheless, I did have a healthy respect for the old lady's faith, and especially for her seemingly intimate relationship with God.

Sitting here forty years later, however hard I strain to remember, I simply cannot recall how John and I and Miss Wilkins happened to be together on that day in the Church of King Charles the Martyr. I must have introduced her to John, I suppose, but I have no idea when or why. I do seem to recall, though, that she had expressed a wish to pray with both of us. Perhaps, to her, this quiet, richly historical place of worship seemed ideal for the purpose.

John and I sat together, I think, side by side on one of the benches. Miss Wilkins stood. She started the proceedings by praying a prayer for all of us, and then she laid her hands on our heads, mine first of all and then John's. While her hands were still on John's head, she began to speak in tongues, the strange gift from God that Paul talks about in the New Testament. I had already witnessed the use of this gift in a few members of my own Anglican church on St John's Road and also in the nearby Pentecostal congregation where I sometimes attended the morning service. At that time I was very unsure about the whole business of spiritual gifts, but I did trust Miss Wilkins and was even beginning to feel quite excited. I knew that the gift of tongues used in public was supposed to be accompanied or followed by another gift, something called "interpretation", either from the person who had spoken in the unknown tongue or from someone else. What might God say to John and I through this spiritually dedicated lady? Yes, looking back I realise that in a quiet sort of way, I really was getting very excited indeed.

I suppose that was what made the actual outcome so upsetting really. God did appear to have something to say to John. Miss Wilkins's interpretation of her own tongue spoke of a future in which he would bring comfort and healing to many. He would be used in all sorts of ways to show the love of God to those who needed it. That came as no surprise to me at all. John had always been loving and warm by nature. Of course God would use him in that way. I would have if I were God.

Now, I said to myself, it's my turn.

But it wasn't. It wasn't my turn. I didn't have a turn. God had nothing to say to me through Miss Wilkins. All there was for me was one great big silence.

Sometimes, if we are not careful, we can fill a silence with the wrong things. I did exactly that after Miss Wilkins had spoken about John. Inside my head I filled it with fear and anger. God had nothing for me in the future. He wanted John, but he didn't want me. I had no future as far as he was concerned. I never had been a Christian, not really. God had taken one look at me and turned his face away in disgust. What else would you expect? All my oldest, deepest insecurities flooded my soul with self-doubt and misery. But I said nothing.

John later became a minister in the Anglican Church and certainly has been all the things that God foretold through Miss Wilkins. For me, the passing of the years meant that the painful memory of that wound faded, but now, four decades later, here in the place where it happened, it has abruptly returned, and the hurt seems to still be there. I do not feel fifty-five. I feel seventeen. I feel raw.

"And you," I cry out from that old juvenile heart of mine, "you nasty cold God, I suppose you still have nothing to say to me."

Yes, I do, says another side of the dialogue in my mind. Actually, I do have something to say. You are not a teenager anymore. You are in your mid-fifties. You make a profession out of telling yourself and others that you are useless, but I want you to think of all the comfort and refreshment that you know full well you have brought to people over the last twenty years, simply by writing honestly about who you are and what I mean to you. Forty years ago you were not ready to hear that these things would happen, and so I did not say them to you. Your wound closed and healed a long time ago. Opening it would be sheer indulgence. The scar is a sign of health. You have reason to trust me now.

I sigh and relax. It is the truth. I am free. I look up at the ceiling once more, thinking about John Doogood and God, these two master craftsmen. I admire the works of their hands.

PART THREE

EXTREME JESUS

Thoughts and Reflections on the Extreme Jesus

CHAPTER 6

AT THE EXTREME EDGE
WITH JESUS

The concept of the "Extreme Jesus" is difficult to explain, not least because the overlap between safety in Christ, an area that we have already discussed, and the freedom to do extreme things for him is inevitable and necessary. It is only when we are truly safe in Christ that we are able to be disinterestedly courageous in the work that he would like us to do as his representatives.

Equally importantly, though, it is difficult because Jesus was and is not actually extreme at all—not, that is, from a divine perspective. All Jesus ever did was what he saw his Father doing. Some of the behaviours that arose from this pattern of living might seem trivial or mundane to us. Others, such as clearing out the temple with a knotted rope or asserting that a dying girl was actually asleep and would soon be awake or being extremely rude to important people, appear dramatic and extreme. In fact, all of these activities, from cooking fish for his followers to embracing the horror of the cross, are symptoms or evidences of a total commitment to obedience. Whatever needed to be done would be done, regardless of how any specific action might appear to human eyes. There is no hierarchy in service. Pleasing God is the priority, and everything else follows on from that.

This part of the book is therefore about our need to accept that we cannot do these apparently extreme things for God unless Jesus really has become the solid ground on which our feet stand. We cannot have one without the other. It has been a desperately hard lesson for me to learn, as you will see from accounts of one or two of my struggles, but it is the same for all of us. Unless and until we begin to genuinely seek the centrality of Jesus in our lives and pray for the courage to set aside personal agendas that never were initiated by the Holy Spirit, we cannot step out and perform the big and little and mild and dramatic and banal and bizarre acts of service that will be required of us. I pray that as you join me on my journey, you will feel personally inspired to reach the place from which all things are possible and to feel affirmed in your own attempts to be "extreme" for Jesus. Be warned though. For most of us it is not an easy road. It will take us to the edge of ourselves, and that is a scary place to be.

JOURNEYING TO THE EXTREME EDGE

I have had a number of encounters with the police, some pleasant, a few very pleasant, and one or two quite decidedly not nice at all. One of the most embarrassing happened nearly twenty years ago when I was in the middle of the stress illness that indirectly resulted in my change of career from residential social worker to writer.

I had arranged to meet a close acquaintance at a café in Eastbourne, but after half an hour at a table by the bow window in this chintzy little establishment, the remains of my second cup of coffee had developed those horrible cream and yellow swirls. It was cold, static, and unappetising. I had also grown weary of craning my neck, peering up and down the road in the hope that I would spot my friend hurrying towards the scene of our increasingly hypothetical rendezvous.

I was beginning to feel very tense. It didn't take much in those days. Where was my so-called friend? Why had he not come? Well, why *hadn't* he? Why was a meeting with me apparently of such minimal importance that this person who was supposed to value me had simply not bothered to turn up? There was something like an emotional kettle inside me, and it was heating up at a ferocious rate. I was in a terrible state and getting worse as the long minutes continued to grind along.

I gave up eventually. Grim, tight-lipped, resentful, I paid for my coffee and walked up the road to find a public telephone. This was the pre-mobile age. I called my wife. Apparently my friend had been in contact only minutes after my leaving the house to say that he wouldn't be able to make it. Some idiotic, flimsy excuse or other. I had been really looking forward to this encounter, and now it wasn't going to happen. Huh! Hardly surprising. Yet more evidence to support a growing if irrational conviction that even the familiar inhabitants of my own little corner of this godforsaken world didn't care.

As I slammed the telephone back onto its stand, that simmering kettle came to a boil. In a moment of blind rage, I drew back my left hand and smashed the flat of my hand against one of the small panes of glass in the wall of the booth with all the force I could muster.

As far as I am aware, there was no specific intention in the act, just a flood of feeling. I hadn't actually intended to break anything. Nevertheless, my blow was responsible for two significant pieces of damage. The first was to the telephone box. The glass panel was completely shattered. The other was to my wrist. I remember gazing with rapt fascination at the gaping wound that had so surprisingly opened up the base of my left hand and asking myself where such a copious flow of blood could possibly be coming from. It was so very red, and there was so much of it. The thought that followed was one I suspect can only be properly understood by those who have been through something similar.

I was pleased.

Deep down in the bottom of my boots, I was pleased. More than that, I was unexpectedly reassured that it was possible to have such an unequivocal outward expression of the inner anguish that was tearing me apart during that phase of my life. It seemed like a proof or confirmation. Even as I write those words, I realise that they must sound a bit silly, but there is nothing I can do about it, I'm afraid. That is how it was. Something visible at last. Something that other people would be able to see.

The manager of a nearby florist's shop called a taxi for me, and within a few minutes I was in the accident and emergency unit of the local hospital having my injury stitched and bandaged. Afterwards, when I returned to the reception area, two policemen were waiting for me. Perhaps the person who called the taxi had, with evenhanded moral and civic responsibility, called the police as well. I never did find out. It doesn't matter very much. These two constables arrested me and said that I would have to accompany them to the police station, where it was possible that I might be charged with criminal damage. (I ought to explain that for some reason, in England you never go anywhere with the police. You always *accompany* them.)

During that brief drive from the hospital to the police station, my hitherto unsuccessful day moved into a faintly surrealistic phase. It transpired that one of the two rather youthful policemen who had been sent to investigate this case of deliberate vandalism was a Christian and a regular viewer of the late-night religious television programme that my wife, Bridget, and I had been regularly involved with for the last couple of years. This young officer's face turned to the colour of half-cooked salmon, presumably as a result of the effort required to inwardly reconcile his reaction to meeting someone who talked about God on the telly with an appropriate professional response to a man who might be guilty of an act of wanton damage. I found those five minutes excruciatingly, maddeningly embarrassing. I like to be in control, but squashed miserably into the back of that car, I wasn't even in control of myself. I felt as though my knowledge of who and what I might be was at sea in a storm and close to being shipwrecked.

AN INSTINCTIVE CRY

The police put me in a cell, the same cell from which I had collected runaway or delinquent children many times in the past in the course of my social work duties. This final irony took me to an even deeper level of humiliation but also, unexpectedly, to a place where I began to understand for the first time the reason those same children had sometimes reacted with such futile violence to bodies such as the police, who were ultimately bound to win all of the short-term battles.

I struggle to find words to describe this sudden moment of comprehension. I discovered that there is a defined genus of rage, or perhaps rather of outrage, erupting from a tear-saturated cloud of disbelief that it is possible to be physically deprived of freedom by people or agencies who have no knowledge of or interest in the aetiology of the act or acts that have brought about the need for restraint. In the case of many children I worked with, there must have been a great silent scream in them that was struggling vainly to be heard behind the very audible swearing and the violent physical resistance that they presented to authority figures such as the police, and sometimes to residential workers like me.

"Do you not understand," their screams might have conveyed if they had ever managed to become articulate, "that this is just a tiny, tiny little incident tacked right on to the very end of fifteen years of confusion and hurt and wondering what love is and wishing and hoping and being disappointed and not being able to say what I mean and getting things wrong? Do you not see that what I really need, what I really, desperately, achingly need, is for someone who has the wisdom and the understanding and the compassion and above all the power and authority to put their arms round me and tell me that they know about the things that were never my fault, and that they forgive the things that were my fault and that they know the difference, and that the future can be different, and that against all the evidence, love simply – well, that it simply is?"

But this is surely not just the cry of teenage children whose lives and hearts have been ploughed into confusion and chaos by the selfishness and inadequacy of those who were supposed to be caring for them. It was my cry as well. And it is the instinctive cry of all those human beings who reach a point in their lives where logic and talent and relationship and habitual role-play are just not working in the same way anymore. It is, of course, a cry to the Father they lack, the Creator, and the one who does actually stand a chance of making a difference in our lives. May God forgive any of us who profess to follow Jesus if we have caused those who are filled with such yearnings to assume that the answer to their profound needs cannot possibly be located in the narrow, twitchy little enclaves that we so casually call church.

It was certainly the cry I sent up from that bleak, unfriendly cell in the police station as I waited to see if I was to be prosecuted by the might of British Telecom, the company who owned the booth that I had damaged. When my fishy-faced, uniformed brother in Christ returned, it was to announce that BT had decided not to press charges as long as I agreed to pay for their property to be repaired. Before I was allowed to leave, though, he had a few statutory things to say about my need to avoid letting bad temper get the better of me, and he rounded off his speech with a warning that if the same thing were to happen again, I would find myself in serious trouble. It was a somewhat flushed and uncomfortable little lecture, but he stuck to his guns and managed it very well. In the end I think he and I were equally relieved that the time had come for me to leave the police station and return to my deeply worried wife.

I have written about this police station incident before, but only in my very first book, published eighteen months or so after the events described. This means that the actual writing must have taken place within a year of my brief incarceration at the hands of the law. There are things about that period and this incident that I understand only in retrospect. They are things I learned about Jesus. Lessons that were shovelled down so far inside me that I was barely aware of their becoming another layer of my awareness. Something about being wounded, particularly in that part of the body. My injury was the foolish outcome of an excessive emotional outburst. His wounds were the marks of sacrifice and love. Of course there is no comparison, and yet I felt that he was allowing an indefinable relationship between his great suffering and my temporary affliction. Sometimes, after the dressing had been taken off and the healing wound on my wrist was exposed to the air, I would find myself staring at the place from which all that blood had flowed and thinking about the love and heroic obedience of Jesus.

"Much more than this," the voice of imagination or delusion, or Jesus, would whisper in my ear at these times, "I would do and have done much more than this for you and for the rest of the sheep who have no shepherd. I am still bleeding for you—for the world. They will not let the bleeding stop. Will you make the shedding of my blood worthwhile? Will you make the shedding of your own blood worthwhile? Give me the wound. Give me all your wounds. Do you dare to do that and let me transfigure them and use them as currency in any way that I choose?"

These were questions that could not possibly be answered with little bleats of "yes" or "no". Certainly not at that time. Besides, I was in no state to offer answers about anything to anyone, human or divine. Life had become one big swirling question. Rather, they were nutrients that entered the veins of my disabled spiritual state, flowing through and contributing to a process of healing that continues as I write these words and is unlikely to be completed before I arrive in heaven.

They are, of course, issues that all of us have to deal with, not just once, whatever anyone may claim loudly from behind one of those transparent lecterns on a platform, but continually. I don't know about you, but I am very good at saying yes when God asks me such questions. Why, I can remember a time when I must have maintained a positive response to a challenge from the Holy Spirit for very nearly an hour. Not bad, eh?

Let us not kid ourselves. Grand gestures from us towards God are pretty meaningless if they are only gestures. Day by day, hour by hour, minute by minute, we need to renew our yes to God. It is a relatively prosaic business most of the time, but why should that put us off? Prose can be very beautiful, and as a very wise man once said, if you stretch monotony far enough, it will break with a sound like a song. This is true in so many areas of our lives. Dedicated and persistent application to the business of prayer or watering plants or teeth-cleaning or exercise or practising a musical instrument can seem wearisome and monotonous at times. There comes a moment, though, when all that discipline and hard work reveal themselves to have been worthwhile.

FOOLS FOR CHRIST

It matters not a jot that we may be stepping out and doing what we consider to be extreme things for God. If our activities, however well meant, constitute something other than Jesus working through us, we may be wasting our time. I suppose it is all about the real nature of humility and our need to be dependent on God, another lesson that I began to learn through the telephone box incident.

We really are not very good at giving up the right to be in control of spiritual initiatives, are we? Simon Peter was a very good example of this. He fiercely declared that he would not allow his Master to be killed. That notion was smartly knocked on the head, and he found himself labelled as "Satan" into the bargain. It wasn't going at all well. At Gethsemane he drew a sword and actually attacked one of the men who had come to capture Jesus, slicing off his ear in the process. That wasn't right either. The sword had to be put away, and the man was given a new ear.

Peter ran out of weapons and ideas all in the same moment. Later, in the courtyard, he learned the terrible truth that, although he had sufficient courage to fight and die for his Master when a sword was involved, he was not brave enough to appear a fool and a loser. He was devastated. I know how he felt.

I see this pattern everywhere, in myself and in others. More or less talented, competent Christians set off on a path that appears perfectly laudable and worthwhile in itself, and may well have been supported or set in motion by God himself. Problems begin when the project fails to move forward in the manner or direction that the worker feels is right and proper. It can be so infuriating to discover that God is not doing the obvious, logical thing when it is required.

"We're doing our part," we cry in exasperation, "so why on earth can't he do his? Surely he can see what's needed. Why doesn't he just get on with it? What is the matter with him? He's supposed to be an omniscient, omnipotent God. Why doesn't he act like one?"

Do you think this sounds extreme or unlikely? I can assure you it is not. I have a friend called Simon, for instance, who, with his wife, runs a quite remarkable church in the north of England. The congregation of this church always reminds me of the story Jesus told about the king who sent out his servants to bring in the poor and the crippled and the blind and the lame from the streets and alleys because none of his invited guests turned up at the wedding feast. The crowd he ended up with must have been a bit like Simon's. It is more of a bus queue than a church, and I love being there. Simon has been faithful and obedient to the call of his Master to go out and bring in the harvest without discrimination. He loves his church, and they love him. So far, so good.

The trouble, and my friend would be the first to admit it, is that God doesn't always seem to follow up on his "successes" in a way that seems right and fitting to Simon. Bridget and I have heard him raging about this quite often in the past.

"I just don't understand it," I can recall him saying as he relaxed in our kitchen one day during a visit. "I *really* don't. We had a couple come to our church earlier in the year. They were into everything. Drugs, booze, sex all over the place with all sorts of people, kids about to be taken into care, a real mess. And the Lord really did something fantastic with that family. Mum and Dad both made commitments and came off the drugs. We had a little service of renewal for their marriage. Tears and singing and – you know – everything.

Kids doing well. Lots of stuff going on. It was wonderful how much they moved forward over a few months. Then, just last week, what do we find? They're both back on drugs, kids not been to school for over a fortnight, and we're practically back to square one." He threw up his hands in despair. "I mean, you tell me where God is in all that, because I certainly don't know! Why has he let that happen?"

It is hard for Simon. God must love him so much. I do. He's such a dynamic human being and deeply, passionately determined to do what God wants, not unlike Simon Peter, I suppose. I wish I had a fraction of his zeal and devotion, and there is not a scrap of humility in that statement. More envy than humility, I'm afraid. I mean it. He works so hard and gives himself so totally to the deprived folk who have seen a possibility of hope through his ministry to them. A wonderful person. He doesn't enjoy a great deal of peace though, because as I have said, God is so chronically bad at sticking to the plan—Simon's plan, that is.

The sad truth that I began to learn in that police cell two decades ago, a truth that has been reinforced many times in the years following, is that God will do what God will do, whatever we may think about it and however passionately we may desire a specific outcome. As our worldly weapons and ploys are revealed to be irrelevant other than at those times when God might happen to need them, we are faced, as Simon Peter was, with the choice of trusting Jesus even in the very centre of apparent failure or giving up and going off to fill our time with some alternative activity such as fishing. Fishing moves smoothly and logically from A to B, even if you don't catch anything, and makes a lot more sense than being a silly old disciple ever has.

Sitting in that police cell, a loser rather than a winner, a baddy rather than a goody, a failure rather than a success, a random blob rather than a design, my self-respect as flat and flabby as a punctured bicycle tyre, I knew one thing for sure. I knew in my heart of hearts or soul of souls, or wherever it is you really know things, that if God did ever, as the result of some gross error of divine judgement, decide that there was a task I could perform for him, I might be willing to put my back into it, but it could not be done in my own spiritual strength, because I had none. I still have none, but I have something else. I am not going to spell out what it is. If you have not identified it by the time you reach the end of this book, then the book will not have been worth writing.

If, by the way, you are wondering why I should describe this truth as a sad one, the answer could not be simpler. You see, I never wanted it to be like that. I understand how Simon feels when he gets so frustrated. Despite agreeing with the proposition that we can do nothing in our own strength and all that, I had actually always longed to do things in my own strength. I wanted to do it, whatever it was, because I was capable of doing it, and I wanted there to be a silent appreciation of that fact. I wanted to own my own virtue and my own good works and have them hanging like pictures on the walls of my public life, set, as it were, in rather attractive frames of humility and self-effacement. I still get a little sad and want that sometimes, but nowadays I feel fairly sure that God's response is to laugh gently at me. I'm glad. It's the best way.

ABSOLUTE TRUST IN JESUS

I have already suggested that safety and extreme obedience overlap, and the place where they come together is in the concept of ultimate trust in Jesus, even in the midst of apparent failure. How crucial it is for the Body of Christ (rather alarmingly, by the way, that is you and me) to consider this issue bravely and clearly. I think I have seen more Western

Christians fall apart because God has "let them down" in some practical way than for any other reason. Disaster strikes in the form of illness, death, or financial ruin, and suddenly the whole business of faith and following Jesus becomes hollow and meaningless.

Why has God let me down? He saw what was going to happen, and he could have prevented it. Why didn't he? Only two possible reasons. Either he doesn't love me after all, or I've been deluding myself and he doesn't exist, in which case it's no use bothering anyway.

It interests me that this response to bad things happening is by no means limited to those whose faith was previously nominal or uncommitted. I know a lady named Janet who for years was a leading light in the most biblical sense, not only in her own church but to many needy people in the village where she lived. She had unusual skills and gifts when it came to caring for those who were hurting for one reason or another, and she was quite open about the fact that her Christian faith motivated and underpinned the work that she did in her community.

Janet was truly wonderful with suffering people, and unlike Simon, she was never discouraged by failure in their lives. On the contrary, she must have dealt with and patiently absorbed their feelings of disappointment and rejection a thousand times, praying and coaxing and gently encouraging these lost souls into understanding why God seemed to have removed his controlling hand from their lives and allowed such dreadful events to strike them.

"It's quite different," Janet was to say to me rather sadly after her own disaster had struck and she had finally recovered a divinely sane perspective, "when you're dealing with other people's troubles. Your own faith seems to grow and get stronger in the face of their difficulties. All sorts of positive arguments and rationalisations pop into your head, and they make so much sense when you're not the one going through it. I don't have any worries about being there to help and comfort people. That was all real. I did genuinely care about them. But when I think of some of the arguments I trotted out so easily. Oh dear ..."

Well, we all know about that, don't we? Theoretical Christianity is so much clearer and easier to comprehend than the real thing. Great fun to talk about sometimes, in fact. My close friends and I have solved most if not all of the problems facing the worldwide church in the course of our long, lazy discussions over a lingering meal or during a walk across the rolling South Downs.

Janet's disaster was twofold. Part of it was to do with money. I never learned exactly what happened, but the outcome was that she lost the comfortable three-bedroom bungalow she loved so much and had to move into a tiny apartment in a part of the town that she previously would have been reluctant to walk through at night, let alone live in. The other calamity in her life, happening within the same short period of time, was the revelation of adultery committed by her pastor with a married woman in the congregation. He was a man she had leaned on heavily for support and for whom she had had enormous respect.

The way in which Janet's faith nose-dived was little short of spectacular. She lost her peace as well. She and my friend Simon would have had no trouble identifying with each other in that respect.

"It doesn't make sense, Adrian," she said dismally. "What am I supposed to do? I'll have to get a full-time job of some sort now, and all the people I see regularly—well, I suppose I'll just have to tell them that I can only see them every now and then. Maybe it would be better if I just gave up my visiting altogether." Pause. "And I can't believe what's happened in the church. I just can't believe it. Nothing seems to mean anything anymore. It's like a big dark cloud coming down over everything. Why would God do this to me, Adrian? What's the point of it?" She became a little tearful. "Have I done something wrong? Maybe I'm being punished. I feel as if Jesus has gone walking crossly on ahead and left me in a little cul-de-sac at the side of the road all on my own."

I have to be honest and say that I was nonplussed by the scale and suddenness of Janet's collapse. She had been one of the reference points in my life. Her existence was a source of refreshment and a place to go when I wanted to reassure myself that it was possible for my chronic scepticism to take a little holiday. I probably trotted out all the usual stuff in her direction, the same list of tidying ploys, no doubt, that Janet herself had used with people in the past. You know the sorts of arguments I mean. We've all heard them. Most of us have used them. Here's a brief selection:

- There's a plan behind it all if we could but see it. One day we shall understand why financial ruin and profound disappointment are actually jolly good things.
- You were doing so many right things that the devil has moved into an open attack on you. Good news seen in perspective!
- Wait and see how wonderfully God can bring good things out of the worst situations.

There's nothing wrong with these arguments, of course; in fact, they are all potentially important and worth considering, but like Janet with her little community of sufferers, I was missing the point, or more accurately, deliberately avoiding it. The questions I really wanted to ask were lodged somewhere at the back of my tongue, and I just couldn't make them come to the front.

"But, Janet," I wanted to say, possibly with the petulance of a disappointed child, "have you never heard of things like this happening to Christians before? You have. You know you have. It happens all the time. Why didn't the things that happened to them make you feel that everything is meaningless? Why didn't you believe in their dark cloud as much as you believe in your own? Did you feel that they might have committed some awful sin and were having to be punished? Of course you didn't! I bet you never let them go on believing any of those things, did you? How can it all have meant so little to you that when financial failure and yet another weak human being falling into sin came along, the spiritual structure of your life came crashing down around your ears?"

Yes, I know what you're thinking, and you are absolutely right. These unspoken questions of mine reveal as much about my own problems as they do about Janet's. But the basic question remains and is valid: Why do we Christians so often find our faith crumpling under the impact of negative events in our lives? Let me put up an answer for you to think about or shoot down or completely ignore if you want. This is it.

We fail partly because of poor teaching and preaching, and partly because it is very frightening and challenging to take on board one of the most fundamental teachings of Jesus, and subsequently of Paul. This is not just one of those pieces of teaching that is mentioned specifically in one, two, or three verses. No, this call to our hearts from the heart of God saturates the pages of the New Testament and is, I know from experience, invisible only to those who choose not to see it.

It is revealed in the words of Jesus about seeking the kingdom of God above all practical need.

It is implicit in the question that Jesus put to the disciples in the boat after they had interrupted his sleep and he had calmed the storm:

> "Why are you so afraid? Do you still have no faith?" (Mark 4:40)

It rings through the Master's words to his disciples in the fourteenth chapter of the gospel of John:

"Do not let your hearts be troubled. Trust in God; trust also in me." (14:1)

And a little further on in the fourteenth chapter:

"Peace I leave with you; my peace I give you. I do not give to you as the world gives. Do not let your hearts be troubled and do not be afraid." (14:27)

It was lived out in the life of the apostle Paul, who wrote:

Are they servants of Christ? (I am out of my mind to talk like this.) I am more. I have worked much harder, been in prison more frequently, been flogged more severely, and been exposed to death again and again. Five times I received from the Jews the forty lashes minus one. Three times I was beaten with rods, once I was stoned, three times I was shipwrecked, I spent a night and a day in the open sea, I have been constantly on the move. I have been in danger from rivers, in danger from bandits, in danger from my own countrymen, in danger from Gentiles; in danger in the city, in danger in the country, in danger at sea; and in danger from false brothers. I have labored and toiled and have often gone without sleep; I have known hunger and thirst and have often gone without food; I have been cold and naked. Besides everything else, I face daily the pressure of my concern for all the churches. Who is weak, and I do not feel weak? Who is led into sin, and I do not inwardly burn? (2 Corinthians 11:23–29)

Paul was following and exemplifying the message of Jesus that trust in him should be an absolute priority, whatever the circumstances we may find ourselves in and however bleak the immediate prospect may appear. And as he points out in the eighth chapter of Romans, we shall eventually discover why this is such a very good idea.

I consider that the sufferings of this present time are not
worth comparing with the glory about to be revealed to us.
(8:18 NRSV)

Stick close to Jesus, and everything else will sort itself out.
The modern church neglects this overwhelming truth at its
peril. The centrality of Jesus has been subject to continual
usurpment by money, buildings, hard work, good works,
Myers-Briggs, efficient organisation, computers, food, the
Bible, church activities, principles, religion, theology, virtue, sex, sexuality, party spirit, meetings, soundness, politics,
fame, talent, tradition, single-issue fanaticism, alcohol, and
family, to name but a few. In his book *Still Higher for the
Highest*, Oswald Chambers expresses this crucial imperative
graphically through a meditation on the passage in the sixth
chapter of Mark's gospel where we read about Jesus walking
on the water:

> If you can stay in the midst of turmoil unperplexed and
> calm because you see Jesus, that is God's plan for your life.
> Not that you may be able to say, "I have done this and that
> and now it's all right". We have an idea that God is leading
> us to a certain goal, a desired haven. He is not. To God the
> question of our getting to a particular end is a mere incident.
> What we call the process, God calls the end. God's purpose
> is that you depend on him and his power now. God's pur-
> pose is that you see him walking on the waves.
> No shore in sight.
> No success.
> Just the absolute certainty that it is all right because you
> see him.

Those two short phrases just before the end of the meditation do rather stand out, don't they? No shore in sight. No
success. How will we live with a challenge as terrifying as
this, especially those of us who are made in such a way that

we measure not just our spiritual worth but our total value by the achievement of specific, hard-won goals? In a funny way it makes me want to weep, the seriousness and the depth of this call from Jesus. "Leave your nets and follow me."

Where to?

To confusion and wonder and ridicule and lots of good meals and fear and rescue and revelation and despair and elation and new friends and fresh enemies and persecution and laughter and a strange sadness and possibly injury and death and certainly something called heaven that will be beyond our wildest imaginings and yet achingly reminiscent of the most beautiful things in this fallen world. To a peace that is not the kind of provisional peace that is ever offered by our circumstances on unredeemed planet Earth. It is a peace that will allow us to be as extreme as God could possibly want us to be.

We must go on working hard to bring people to a faith in Jesus. We are to be his hands and feet and voice in the community, local and global, bringing practical help and assistance to those who need it. We Christians need to be pastors and evangelists and teachers and comedians and police officers and greengrocers and writers and theologians and street cleaners and makers of stained-glass windows and prayer warriors and unemployed and jobbing gardeners and anything else that might be useful, but I am convinced that if our lives are not hidden away in Christ, as the Bible puts it, then the storm winds of misfortune may knock us flat and leave us helpless, and we don't want that, do we?

Do we?

I have known and met people, as you probably have, who exemplify this capacity for remaining safe and strong because the source of that safety and strength is Jesus himself, as opposed to material security or success in religious projects. When I was a much younger man, such people used to annoy me a little, possibly because my frail psyche fed on an exclusive diet of indigestible negatives for a time. There was something unsettling and subtly alienating about people who genuinely did find their solid ground in a relationship with Jesus. In a way they were like creatures from another planet, breathing a different air. I certainly wanted what they seemed to have, but I seriously doubted that I would be willing to pay the price when it was required of me, and I secretly feared that I would, in any case, fail to qualify for whatever it was they had. It was a bit like poor old insecure Charlie Brown wanting to be rich and famous and humble.

Nowadays I rejoice when I encounter these loving souls with an unfathomable depth of hurt and peace in their eyes. They show me what is possible and remind me that for all of the silliness with which some of our religious structures are infected, there is clean spiritual health available to the sick of this world. The price is worth paying, and as I have an advanced degree in being a lost human being who needs to be saved, I am quite sure that I qualify.

So my brief sojourn in a police cell was quite productive and helpful, was it not? But, you may want to ask, what is the practical outcome of all these reflections and conclusions? Good question. The answer is simple but actually very profound. It will become clear by the time you read through the next chapter. I hope to see you there.

CHAPTER 7

FALLING THROUGH TO SOLID GROUND

L et me tell you about something that happened in our family eighteen months ago, and I will do my very best to be honest about how it affected me. It was the middle of summer, and Bridget and I had gone to bed with the electric fan switched on at the foot of our bed because, amazingly for this country, we were passing through a very hot spell.

At about three o'clock in the morning, the telephone rang. As many of you will know, it is hard to imagine a more alarming sound. At that dreadful, heart-stopping hour of the morning, the noise of a ringing telephone corkscrews its way into the core of your dreams, dragging consciousness back through the narrow passage between sleep and waking like a cork being drawn from a bottle.

We both woke, but the telephone was on Bridget's side. There was a breathless fear in her voice when she asked who was there. Filled with apprehension myself, I waited. Our history of receiving calls in the early hours had not been a positive one. It might have been an American friend who never had been very good at geography or mathematics, but usually it was bad news.

That was what it was this time. Very bad news. Our twenty-three-year-old second son, Joe, who lived twenty-odd miles along the coast from us in Brighton, had fallen from a height of thirty feet and was now in the hospital, severely injured. Severely injured? What did that mean? How severely? What injuries? Was he going to live? Something to do with his leg and his wrist, the policeman on the phone told us, possibly other complications. He was alive at the moment.

Alive at the moment.

As we threw on our clothes and located the car keys, a sick dread seemed to rise in me like vomit. Joe and I have had our battles over the years, but I love him fiercely. The thought of losing him was like a dark blind being pulled down over a source of light in my heart. The journey to Brighton along bleakly, blessedly deserted roads beneath the sulphurous light of interminable necklaces of streetlamps was a filmic nightmare of tension and dark imaginings.

Bridget and I react very differently when things like this happen. My wife's feelings rise to the surface instantly and are given full expression. I become unnaturally still and calm. Sometimes I wish we could exchange skins. I know our dominant fear was precisely the same though. Would Joe still be alive when we arrived at the hospital?

He was alive, but only just. We found him lying on one of the emergency trolleys that we had seen so often in hospital dramas on the television. There was no music though, and the script was halting and poor.

A group of five or six doctors and nurses surrounded him, deep in an intense discussion about what sort of technical procedures were indicated. We soon discovered why so many people were involved. Joe was in a terrible state. His jaw was fractured in several places. His left wrist was, to quote the doctor examining him at the time, destroyed. His left femur had snapped in two. Because of trauma and shock, he was breathing only with enormous difficulty.

We hovered helplessly on the edge of this dreadful scene, our whole beings filled with one overwhelming question that we did not dare to ask. We couldn't actually lay hands on him, of course, but we did reach towards him with our hands and our hearts, sending out silent, urgent, inchoate prayers for his healing.

The next two or three days and nights seemed like a dry run for eternity. Joe lay unconscious in the intensive care unit, battling for his life, his breathing being done by a machine, while we spent most of our time with his girlfriend, Hannah, and her mum in the little waiting area outside, consuming endless cups of coffee that we didn't really want, jumping convulsively every time someone came through the ward doors in case they were bringing news of his condition.

Every now and then we were allowed to spend some time at his bedside. All around us in this hushed place, machines buzzed and clicked as they supported lives that were hanging by a thread. Incredibly, our son was one of them. As far as we knew, he was barely aware of our presence. Nevertheless, I made a point of whispering the cricket scores into his ear, a conversational priority that can only be properly understood by the mad English. Our national team had done well for once. The shock of learning that an England team has come close to winning anything at cricket is enough to revive or finally finish off anyone, let alone an avid fan like Joe.

Close proximity to an ICU takes one into a world of wildly swinging, intense emotions and moments. At irregular intervals relatives and friends of those who were being treated in the ward would come out through those double doors exhibiting all possible levels of emotion, from enormous relief to utter devastation. You could see it in every line of their bodies. I am sure we were exactly the same. I suppose, at its best, it created a little community of suffering, but there was only a tissue-thin gap between the best and the worst. I think we would rather have seen no one.

He lived. He recovered. At last he began to breathe on his own. The surgeon who put twenty-eight screws into Joe's shattered jaw said that he had never seen a worse case and never done a better job. The destroyed wrist gradually regained much of its movement, and the fingers that he might "never be able to use again" returned very nearly to normal. Joe's left leg is now a few millimetres shorter than his right, but as he is now playing soccer regularly once more on Monday evenings, it can't be too much of a handicap, can it?

Thank God for all that.

Don't ask me if any miracles were involved in the amount of healing that happened. I don't know. I have no idea. A lot of people prayed consistently and faithfully for his recovery, and there certainly were one or two unexpectedly dramatic forward steps in his progress. If God laid his hand on Joe in any specific way, I am endlessly grateful. On the other hand, I know that a number of highly skilled and dedicated people worked long and hard to make Joe better, and I am a long way from seeing clearly where dedication and skill end and miracles begin. From the bottom of my heart I thank God for all those doctors and nurses.

I am only too aware also that many Christians and relatives of Christians do not recover from illness and accident, however fervently and devotedly they may be prayed for and whatever hysterical preachers may say in support of their single-issue fanaticism. There are no guarantees. No success. No shore in sight. Just the knowledge that Jesus is there.

So, having offered this brief summary of what happened to my son, and having tacked the odiously pious bit on the end, back to the reason for telling the story in the first place. How did I react? What did this near disaster do to my faith? What was passing through my mind and spirit as I stood in the accident and emergency unit at three thirty in the morning, staring at Joe's shattered body and wondering if he would ever speak to me again in this world?

Some things are very private, aren't they? One thing I am beginning to learn, though, is that God very rarely gives us anything that is not for sharing with others. It applies to everything from money to miracles. Against a proper awareness that pearls are not intended for distribution to swine, I suspect we must balance the undoubted fact that misers are neither popular nor useful in the kingdom of God. If you are a swine, you could always skip to the next page.

SIMPLE BUT SIGNIFICANT

Still here? Good. So how did I feel? Well, do you know that feeling of falling through the holes in your own life? I imagine a fair number of people would understand what that means. Most of us have been through it at one time or another. You can fall through the holes in your finances or your relationships or your faith or your marriage or your church or your health. Just about anything and everything, really. That is what happened to me as I gazed at the bruised and swollen face of my beloved son. A sensation of spiritual vertigo sent me spiralling downwards. What were the holes that I fell through? I shall have to think carefully about that for a moment.

In the small but useful gap between the last paragraph and this one, I've thought. The holes I fell through were gaps in any organised understanding of the Christian faith. Gaps in the endless collections of words with which I and others have attempted to corral the wild horses of power and love that thunder through this world of ours and will not be tamed and ridden by mere men and women. Gaps in the certainty with which I have sometimes falsely addressed groups of people when my nerve is gone, and I have forgotten who Jesus is, and my own doubts and fears have seemed a poor offering to lay before folk who seem so needy. Gaps in the ridiculously proud assurance that God and I are buzzing along in tandem, bringing succour to a fallen world. Huge, ragged gaps in any sense of being grown up and competent and responsible and able to cope with anything, except as a very small child copes, by crying until somebody comes. Gaping chasms in the game, the artifice, the humanly assembled infrastructure of the thing we call "being a Christian".

Where did I land after falling through all these holes? Ah, there is the question that is so fundamentally important, not just to me, but to all of us. Where do we land? Where do you land? My own answer was filled with a peculiar cocktail of embarrassment and relief. Embarrassment because it was such a basic, old-fashioned place on which to find my feet. Relief because I had not plummeted to such a depth that I found myself on my own in some dismally echoing pothole or cavern of nothingness.

I landed in a place where I knew that Jesus had died so that my sins could be forgiven. That was it. That was all. Very simple. Hugely significant. Good old tin-tabernacle stuff, isn't it? That was where my feet found solid ground, and that was what saved me from an even longer fall. It was enough.

I felt no inclination or desire to blame God or to wonder why he had allowed Joe to fall thirty feet from the top of some scaffolding—that had immeasurably more to do with Joe than with God—nor did I feel that in some way I was owed my son's recovery. He might live, or he might die. I was certainly not given any assurances on that score. What God did give me on that terrible morning, however, was an unobtrusive but profoundly supportive realisation that the miracle of redemption, of being saved by Jesus (whatever that finally turns out to mean), is sufficient indication that dear old Julian of Norwich was right when she said that "all things would be well", and even more comfortingly, that "all manner of things would be well".

In case you think I might be making out the case for my own sainthood, I ought to add that for most of my Christian life, this reaction would not have been possible. And it was not the result of deep devotional prayer and rigorous study. I wish I could say it was. It had far more to do with a profound need the child in me has for a Father he can depend on, and a weary submission to the plainly evident fact that like Simon Peter, my own attempts to "move forward spiritually" with God leave me so battered by failure that I am eventually forced into believing Jesus when he says that we should lay our burdens on him. I recommend it. I truly do. By so doing you may reveal what a twit you always were, but it's so much less of a strain.

A DOWNWARDS SPIRAL

Perhaps this "falling through the holes" experience should be introduced as one of the rides in a Christian theme park. It might encourage people to let themselves go when the real thing happens. And just in case you think this applies only to major incidents, I ought to say that it had already happened to me in church one Sunday morning a year or so before the business with Joe. It will sound trivial and silly in comparison, but in a way it was just as important to me. It was to do with two things, my critical attitude and my trousers, the latter being an area very rarely covered in ministry, as I am sure you are aware.

It was just that as I sat there in church on the end of a row as usual, I suddenly looked at these two aspects of myself, one on the inside and one on the outside, and realised how shabby both of them were, and how boringly predictable that state had become.

The trousers first. I have always hated shopping for clothes, and especially trousers. I flail desperately around, hopping on one leg (come to think of it – you can't hop on two legs, can you?) in those tiny, inadequately curtained changing cubicles that are designed for exhibitionist midgets, panicking and crashing against the flimsy walls and failing miserably to fit the unsuitable pairs back into their plastic hanger things after I've tried them on and found that they only come halfway up my calves. It may be because of my shape. All right, the truth may embarrass me, but it will also set me free. It *is* because of my shape. When the new heaven and the new earth have been sorted out, trousers will fit me because they will be trousers of the new order. Meanwhile, in my untransfigured state, I am not made for trousers, and trousers have quite definitely never been made for me. For this reason, if I discover a pair that almost seem to fit, I utter a sigh of relief and buy them instantly. I then wear them forever, or until fragmentation is so imminent that the tiny cubicles have to be braved once more.

A journalist accompanied me on a tour of Holland once in order to be able to write a piece for a Dutch newspaper. In the finished article he mentioned a number of my more negative personal characteristics. Being a redeemed child of God, I wasn't hurt and offended, of course – well, only to the extent of wanting to boil the journalist in oil just a little bit before forgiving him, but I was obscurely depressed by a reference he made to my "strange green trousers". It hung over me like a small dark cloud for some time. I can pretend to handle criticism about the depth and quality of my writing, my personality, and my ministry, but when a man attacks your trousers – well, that's another matter.

The tendency to become judgemental in church services is left over from those days when my self-respect demanded that everyone and just about everything had to be submerged so that this frail ego of mine could stay afloat. I think I have described this ugly phenomenon elsewhere in these pages. I no longer allow such foolishness to take up residence in my will, but the ghost of it drags me down sometimes like a phantom limb after an amputation. This time it formed an unholy alliance with the latest in a long line of shabby pairs of trousers that I happened to be wearing and turned me into one long, deep sigh of fed-upness. Nothing changes much, I thought miserably. What was the point of living?

You think the trousers are a bit of an exaggeration? No, not really. In my mind they had become a sort of symbol of negative things about myself that never really seem to change. Some of us Christians are funny little people. We may be aware that God is mighty and all-loving and all-forgiving and all the rest of it, and very glad and grateful we are too, but it doesn't stop us from being temporarily defeated by our own weaknesses, even if some of them are only vestiges. Please don't send me letters ministering to my failure in these areas. You'll only be doing it to make yourself feel better. Jesus and I and my wife and our church and a couple of friends are managing nicely, thank you very much.

Anyway, the point I was making was that the same downward spiralling thing happened with trousers and intolerance as happened when Joe had his accident (okay, yes, I suppose it is true that I fell through the hole in my trousers, but I'm trying to be serious here), and I landed in the same place. Jesus died for me. He loves me, and because of that nothing else matters very much. Not very high-powered on the face of it, but jolly good theology.

And this is so important, don't you think? So necessary to learn the value of this retreat to first essentials when dark things crowd in on us, whether they involve sitting in a police cell, death, injury, trousers, or sin. And we are certainly not talking about some abstract, ethereal proposition that has no real impact on our daily lives. On the contrary, if we do not incorporate this principle into our walk with Jesus, how will we ever survive continual and inevitable confrontations with our own weaknesses and shortcomings?

Paul summed it up in a passage that has acted as a lifeline to many Christians, including me. It comes from the epistle to the Romans. Read it and have a good think about what it might really mean:

> We know that the law is spiritual; but I am unspiritual, sold as a slave to sin. I do not understand what I do. For what I want to do I do not do, but what I hate I do. And if I do what I do not want to do, I agree that the law is good. As it is, it is no longer I myself who do it, but it is sin living in me. I know that nothing good lives in me, that is, in my sinful nature. For I have the desire to do what is good, but I cannot carry it out. For what I do is not the good I want to do; no, the evil I do not want to do – this I keep on doing. Now if I do what I do not want to do, it is no longer I who do it, but it is sin living in me that does it.
>
> So I find this law at work: When I want to do good, evil is right there with me. For in my inner being I delight in God's law; but I see another law at work in the members of my body, waging war against the law of my mind and making me a prisoner of the law of sin at work within my members. What a wretched man I am! Who will rescue me from this body of death? Thanks be to God – through Jesus Christ our Lord!
>
> So then, I myself in my mind am a slave to God's law, but in the sinful nature a slave to the law of sin. (7:14–25)

The argument gets a bit convoluted, rather like the instructions in one of those self-assembly furniture packs, but the message is clear. And it also might be useful to reflect on that verse in the first epistle of John, where the writer, probably John the cousin of Jesus, tells us that if anyone does sin, Jesus will speak to the Father in our defence (2:1). Think of that!

How does my experience of "falling through the holes" relate to the extreme Jesus? Well, I think it is fair to say that the place on which our feet find solid ground in such a situation is the place from which we truly operate as human beings. When it is Jesus who keeps us steady, we are steady indeed, steady enough to go to any lengths or extremes for God because the ground will not–cannot–crumble beneath our feet. At one time or another and for many different reasons, we are all likely to fall through the holes in our lives. I pray that we will discover we have landed in the place of true strength, and that our discovery will inspire us to be brave, bold, and extreme for Jesus.

CHAPTER 8

STEPPING OUT
WITH JESUS

Do you want to be the hands and feet of Jesus, taking the extremes of his love and judgement and warning and compassion to a needy world? I feel quite sure that you will answer in the affirmative, and you will mean it. I am equally sure, though, that many of those who read this book feel burdened and incapacitated by the weight of their own sins. Let us be quite clear about this. We cannot stand shoulder to shoulder with Jesus, ready and able to represent him in all the boring or bizarre situations that we encounter, while we are unhealthily obsessed with our own shortcomings. At its worst this is an obscure form of vanity. And it cripples so many of us believers. As a church we seem to have forgotten that Christianity is a positive faith, not a negative one. It is more about doing the good and useful things than avoiding the bad ones. How can we begin to redress the balance in our own lives?

THE OBSTACLE OF SIN

In the course of travelling and speaking to people over the last twenty years, I have met thousands of Christians who cannot get past the obstacle of their own sins. Of course they can't.

They want to be perfect for God, but every single day reveals how far they fall short of their aim. I would suggest that the solution to this problem begins with the tough but necessary business of accepting our own sinful natures. Now, before someone rings the heresy police and they swoop down to carry me off for interrogation and torture (in love, of course), let me make it quite clear that I am not even putting my toe in the edge of the outgoing tide of talking about condoning sin. In Paul's epistle to the Romans, he says: "What shall we say, then? Shall we go on sinning so that grace may increase? By no means! We died to sin; how can we live in it any longer?" (6:1–2).

No, I have no wish whatsoever to meet the great apostle just inside the gates of heaven and have him go on and on at me about giving people the idea that sin is all right. I know we shall be perfect in heaven, but a perfect Paul might still be capable of giving newly arrived half-baked Christian writers a tongue-lashing. No, what I am trying to say is that although we co-operate with the Holy Spirit in changing our lives, working very hard to be obedient, it is Jesus who has died so that our sins can be forgiven–not us. There is no effort we can make, no penance we can perform that will bring us any closer to being forgiven than the sacrifice that Jesus has already made.

There is, as I have said, a subtle and somehow typically human vanity in the notion that God cannot accept me because there is still sin in my life. If that is my belief, then I have missed the point entirely. God hates sin because it has ruined his relationship with the world he loves, but at the risk of incurring thunderbolts, I would say that in the case of many of his followers, he is less concerned with their sin than with their priorities. And this brings us back to the idea of that ideal place of trust in Jesus, the place where there is no shore in sight, no prospect of success, occasional waves of sin, and a sense of absolute safety in him. That place where all the demands of God, however extreme, are not just possible but highly likely to happen.

OUR SINS AND JESUS

There are lots of sins in my life. Shall I tell you about some of them? I can get quite unpleasantly irritable and grumpy, but usually only with people who are close to me because I know they'll forgive me later on. I fantasise unhealthily about all sorts of things and people. Hard luck if you want details – look at your own fantasies. I tell lies, many different kinds of lies, mainly subtle and disguised ones, but a few are quite blatant. What else? I'm going to stop typing for a moment and go into the kitchen, where my wife and daughter are making pancakes, and ask them what my main sins are.

I'm back. I didn't get so much as a square inch of pancake, and it was a bit difficult getting through to them, but I did observe my wife's incredulity when I asked her that perfectly straightforward question, and I did receive her considered opinion that if I'm finding it difficult to assemble a list of my sins, there must be something seriously wrong with me. She also suggested that I have a recurring tendency to bully and become intolerant towards others when I think they're deluding themselves. Nonsense! What rubbish! I told her what I thought about that ridiculous view in no uncertain terms.

What else? Laziness sometimes, a capacity for wasting time that can result in my having to work frenetically hard to catch up, thus giving the impression to onlookers that I am actually the opposite of idle. It would be sad to disabuse those trusting souls, wouldn't it?

Then there's good old pride, a constant companion in my case. Just this week, for instance, a man from one of the local churches came round to our house to discuss something and in the course of our conversation started telling me what, in his opinion, was wrong with one of the ministers in our town. Bridget and I have a fixed policy for dealing with negative gossip nowadays. We always respond by listing positive aspects of the person who is being rubbished. It's a good idea, even if it does spoil the conversation and seriously irritate the other person. I did it this time. That was all right, but after the man had gone, I found myself glowing like a beacon with my own righteousness and was forced to confess to God, who had happened to be present during the conversation, that I was no better than my visitor. You can't win, can you? But he can, or rather has, I'm pleased to say.

Some sinful areas of my life are much more vague and, oddly, more distressing. At times, especially when I feel threatened, I am appalled by a sudden overall reduction in the quality of my own character. A cheap, loud, rather thoughtless person emerges and makes bad mistakes in his dealings with others. Does that person really live there inside me, I find myself wondering, or is he just an occasional visitor? Not very nice.

Most immediately distressing, perhaps, are those sins of cruelty that result in our attacking the people dearest to us. Close as we are, Bridget and I are aware that we both reserve our most hurtful comments for each other, and it is so difficult to take back those stinging, destructive words with which we lash out when we are emotionally cornered. Some of the very worst times in my life have been those wretched moments when I have risen to my feet to address a crowd, knowing that I have just caused a deep and painful rift in a relationship that is one of the most precious I shall ever know.

This can be a real problem for so-called Christian speakers. God grants me no greater immunity from being human and vulnerable than anyone else, and I have to work hard to keep in balance the tension between everything that I am and everything that God is. I cried out to God once that I was sick to my stomach with falling so far short of being able to match my message. A little dialogue began in my mind. One end of it was certainly me. I have always believed that the other end was God, but of course I may be wrong. What it said was this:

"Okay, you go off into a little corner and tell yourself how rotten and useless you are if that gives you any satisfaction. Feel as sorry for yourself as you like. Despise yourself if you want. Beat yourself up to within an inch of your life. But don't you ever, ever dare to despise what I do through you, because that is completely different."

"Yes, well—all right, then. Err, sorry . . . "

Back to sins. There are probably lots of other sins I can't or don't want to remember at the moment. All in all I must have broken every one of the Ten Commandments, either in practice or in my head, the latter being just as bad according to Jesus. Do you remember these two passages from the gospel of Matthew?

> "You have heard that it was said to the people long ago, 'Do not murder, and anyone who murders will be subject to judgment.' But I tell you that anyone who is angry with his brother will be subject to judgment, Again, anyone who says to his brother, 'Raca,' is answerable to the Sanhedrin. But anyone who says, 'You fool!" will be in danger of the fire of hell." (5:21–22)

> "You have heard that it was said, 'Do not commit adultery.' But I tell you that anyone who looks at a woman lustfully has already committed adultery with her in his heart." (5:27–28)

Troubling stuff, eh? Unless, that is, Jesus is kindly sorting things out for us with his Father. Do you believe he is? I believe it fifty-seven and a half percent of the time.

You may be amused and interested to hear, by the way, that when I mentioned this business of having broken all the commandments during a talk in my own church once, I was buttonholed afterwards by a mild, troubled-looking man who thought I was saying that I had physically and actually broken all ten of these fundamental laws of God. He was greatly relieved when I explained that while, for instance, I had not actually slaughtered anyone with my bare hands, there had been one or two folk in my life I would quite like to have murdered, and certainly one or two I had considered fools. He seemed to think that was all right. He obviously didn't think it necessary to ask me about stealing or adultery. I wasn't sure whether to be insulted or flattered.

Mine is not really a very impressive list of shortcomings, is it? Nothing very juicy. There used to be one or two more interesting items, but nowadays it is rare for me to commit anything that you might conceivably label "original" sin – if I may put it like that. Each of the weaknesses I have is a door of temptation through which, from time to time, I must choose to go or not go. Hopefully, as the years go by, some of those potential gateways to less than admirable behaviour are becoming dusty and rusty and covered in spiders' webs through disuse. That is certainly what the Trinity and I are working on.

I must admit that some are taking rather longer than others, but there has been major improvement in one or two directions. Sulking, for instance, is something that used to be a dominant feature in my relationships, but recent years have seen this very destructive tendency wither and almost die, thank God. In one sense this is rather a shame. I have few enough areas of expertise as it is. Though I say it myself, I was quite an ace exponent of the art of sulking. I have mentioned elsewhere my famous shuddering sigh, which needs to be delivered to one's partner just as she is turning away.

Catching the tail end of this pathetic sound, she asks with real alarm, "What on earth is the matter?"

"Nothing," I reply brokenheartedly.

Yes, I could have run weekend seminars for husbands on the art of sulking and made a lot of money, but then we are asked to give sacrificially as Christians, aren't we?

PARTNERS WITH JESUS

Changing some aspects of my behaviour has been very hard work, and I think it might be worth repeating the point that while forgiveness is the exclusive province of our heavenly Father, the work of change is the result of a partnership between Jesus and me – or you. How does that statement grab you? Does it make you feel a little uneasy? Does it challenge an oft-repeated strand of teaching that says that only God can change us and we can do nothing in or of ourselves? Is it heresy?

You know, there is not much genuine rage in me nowadays, but I maintain a small store to draw from when necessary, and I suspect that the Holy Spirit tops it up periodically. In my view there is not enough appropriate anger in the church today. A significant portion of this intense fury of mine is reserved for teachers and preachers who seem to specialise in bewildering and bamboozling the children of the kingdom. I'm sure you know the ones I mean.

For a start they only have problems in the past, never in the present. They ignore Jesus' teaching about cost and offer conversion as though it were like one of those store cards, one small, effortless prayer as a deposit and after that you can take as much as you want without paying. They teach that Christianity is not about formulae and then make sure that you have learned that principle word for word.

Most important, in the context of what we have been talking about, their teaching says that although change is essential, you and I can't do it, only God can do it, and then when you and I find that nothing happens and we haven't changed and we can't do it, they raise a censorial eyebrow and announce that it must be our fault. Most of us would rather be thrown back into the waters from which they fished us than flop helplessly around in the pathetically limited confines of their suffocating, strangling nets.

Do you think I sound judgemental? Ah, well, what you have to understand is that it's prophetic rather than personal. That's my excuse. Thank goodness God loves them. I don't, and therefore I must. I would like to shower them with damp and clammy texts, like emptying a barrel of eels over their heads, if it weren't for the fact that I know how pointless and annoying it is because they have so often done the same to me. One longish quotation from the gospel of Luke will do for now, where Jesus says:

> "If anyone comes to me and does not hate his father and mother, his wife and children, his brothers and sisters – yes, even his own life – he cannot be my disciple. And anyone who does not carry his cross and follow me cannot be my disciple.
>
> "Suppose one of you wants to build a tower. Will he not first sit down and estimate the cost to see if he has enough money to complete it? For if he lays the foundation and is not able to finish it, everyone who sees it will ridicule him, saying, 'This fellow began to build and was not able to finish.'
>
> "Or suppose a king is about to go to war against another king. Will he not first sit down and consider whether he is able with ten thousand men to oppose the one coming against him with twenty thousand? If he is not able, he will send a delegation while the other is still a long way off and will ask for terms of peace. In the same way, any of you who does not give up everything he has cannot be my disciple." (14:26–33)

You might also like to read the fourteenth and fifteenth chapters of John's gospel, taking close note of the frequency and passion with which Jesus talks about the need for obedience. Why not read them right now?

Do you get the impression from all of this that our role is a passive one? No, of course you don't, and neither do I. As well as being all the other things that it is, following Jesus is very hard work, and sometimes the weight of the cross that we are asked to carry can seem intolerable. We Christians live with the fact that while spiritual initiatives come from God, we are called upon to carry out the tasks he appoints to us with everything that we have and are. Still want to be extreme?

To put it more simply, once we know what God wants us to do, we need to get on with it and do it with all our might. "Feed my sheep," Jesus said to Peter once the big fisherman had given up churning out his own ideas, and that is exactly what Peter did.

BEING THE HANDS AND FEET OF JESUS

I could, I suppose, continue by listing my virtues. I have decided not to do that because it would take up too much of the book, but in one very important and serious sense, there is no point. Neither the bad nor the good things that I do are relevant to the gift of forgiveness that Jesus has freely given me, and in any case, I need to make the vital point that the kinds of sin I have just listed are not and never were the important ones.

Throughout its history too many sections of the Christian community have majored on negative issues and thus portrayed themselves to the rest of the world as weak and irrelevant. I cannot imagine anything more boring and ineffectual than a church that is concerned only with making sure that its members do not do "bad things". Do you remember this passage in Matthew's gospel?

> Hearing that Jesus had silenced the Sadducees, the Pharisees got together. One of them, an expert in the law, tested him with this question: "Teacher, which is the greatest commandment in the Law?"
>
> Jesus replied, " 'Love the Lord your God with all your heart and with all your soul and with all your mind.' This is the first and greatest commandment. And the second is like it: 'Love your neighbor as yourself.' All the Law and the Prophets hang on these two commandments." (22:34–40)

Wonderful, isn't it? Jesus certainly did not come to abolish the law, but he did come to put it in its place and express it in a new way. All the negative injunctions that we associate with Moses are subsumed in these two most positive of commandments. If we are coming anywhere near to obeying in these two areas, we are bound to see the beginnings of change and improvement and excitement in the way we conduct our lives. As we have already said, Christianity is supposed to be about what we do, not just about avoidance of traditional sin. Understanding this presents us with an alarming challenge and a much more dynamic and possibly disturbing understanding of what is meant by sin.

In John's gospel Jesus says this:

> "I tell you the truth, the Son can do nothing by himself; he can do only what he sees his Father doing, because whatever the Father does the Son also does." (5:19)

These words always have the same effect on me. They remind me that the part of my life that is most given over to wrongdoing has little to do with sins of commission, as we pompous Anglicans call them, but with sins of omission, those occasions when something should have happened, but it didn't, because I didn't do it. What has that to do with the passage I just quoted? Let me try to explain.

Jesus was without sin. I believe that. And yet, as I have said elsewhere, he caused his parents great concern when he was just a boy, he violently ejected traders from the temple courtyard, he called one of his closest followers "Satan", he made what sounds very much like a racist comment to a Greek woman who was asking for help, he was extremely abusive to important members of the community, he publicly disowned his own family, he cursed a fig tree that subsequently died, he didn't do anything to save his cousin John when he was imprisoned by Herod, and hanging on the cross, he seemed to have lost faith in his Father altogether.

Despite all these "extreme" things, he was without sin. As I have said, I really do believe that. Unfortunately, the teaching of Jesus has been hijacked by those whose priority has become safety through respectability. In fact, they are not safe, and their "keeping your nose clean" culture has provided a breeding ground for serious error and for pharisaic attitudes that are bound to repel or confuse those who have sensed the glory of God and want to be authentic followers of Jesus.

Jesus was a lover of Scripture, he quoted it continually, but he had no book of rules for dealing in detail with the situations that faced him during his ministry. He only did what he saw his Father doing. That is the challenge that constantly faces and frightens us. Will we be ready and willing to be the hands and feet and voice of Jesus in any situation? Will we keep our mouths shut when there is every reason to speak except for the most important one of all? Will we open our mouths and say the things that need to be said, however much they may expose us to ridicule or even hatred? Are we prepared to abandon our very human desire for pattern and consistency? Will we, by an act of the will, step away from the limited options of stereotyped Christian reactions and behaviours so that we can do what we see the Father doing, as opposed to conforming to impotently mild and defensive expectations, or retreating because of fear?

MY TRAIN JOURNEY

Sometimes I have overcome my fear and done *it*, whatever it is, or tried to do it. On these occasions the results have sometimes been fascinating. Much more often, however, I have not done the thing I fear. I have been a terrible coward at times, and the thought of it makes me feel very ashamed, depressed, and angry with myself. It occurs to me even as I write that I had an experience on the night before last that was definitely one of the "not" occasions. I don't want to write about it or even think about it, but I can see how relevant it is, so I suppose I must.

I was travelling back by train from London to Polegate, our nearest railway station, after a meeting in London. It was cold and dark and late. Because of a shortage of carriages, my train didn't actually begin its eighty-minute journey from Victoria Station until after eleven o'clock in the evening. Very few passengers got on at Victoria, and there was only one other person in my part of the train, a well-dressed elderly man who appeared to have fallen asleep as soon as he relaxed back in his seat by the door at one end of the carriage.

I alternately dozed and read a newspaper until the train came to a halt at Haywards Heath Station. A group of four or five people opened the door nearest to me and climbed from the platform into my carriage, occupying places out of sight on the other side of the seat in front of me. Two of the young men seemed a little noisy, but I hardly noticed what they looked like as they got on. Within a couple of minutes the train had lurched into motion again, and I resumed my reading and dozing as before.

I was jerked back into full consciousness when a young fellow in his early twenties, presumably one of the group that had got on at the last station, plonked himself heavily down on the seat next to me and after a pause of a few seconds turned his head and addressed me raucously:

"Excuse me, mate," he said, "but do you think it's fair that one bloke, who's supposed to be your friend, right? Is it fair that he takes the mickey out of you just because you're wearing a different coat from the one what he's wearing? D'you think that's fair? When he's s'posed to be your mate, I mean."

Looking into the eyes of my new companion, I detected the unmistakable combination of vacancy and wobbling concentration that commonly results from the excessive absorption of one or more intoxicating substances. The "coat" issue was typically random and impossible to answer, but why had he decided to confide in me?

"Well," I responded feebly, "these things do happen."

At this point a leering, lolling head appeared over the top of the seat in front of me. It was like some grotesque puppet show. The saucering eyes and wildly grinning mouth suggested that this person had matched and overtaken the young man next to me in his consumption of something or other.

"That's 'im!" shouted my neighbour, pointing a wavering finger in the direction of the head. "That's the one who took the mickey out of me because of my coat! Go on, tell 'im what you think of 'im!"

I was beginning to feel very uneasy. When I am travelling with a companion, and especially with my wife or daughter, my reactions tend to be very different. I simply feel protective. On my own it is not the same. There were two or three more of these unstable individuals on the other side of that seat. Suppose they all turned nasty, all at the same time, and decided to make me the object of their aggression. I had opened my mouth and was about to say something weak and noncommittal to the owner of the head when he forestalled me with the following question:

"How old d'you think I am?"

Oh no, I groaned to myself. Here we go. One of those questions that doesn't have a right answer, not in situations like this, anyway. If I guess he's much older than he really is, he'll tell me I'm deliberately getting at him. If I'm wildly wrong in the other direction, the same thing will happen.

"Tell 'im what you think of 'im!" repeated the man on my left. "Tell 'im to stop takin' the mickey out of my coat. Go on!"

"I'm fifty-five!" said the head triumphantly.

At this the man beside me went into peals of maniacal laughter, repeating the number fifty-five over and over again as though it were the best joke in the world. Then there was a lull. They both looked at me. I licked my lips and swallowed with some difficulty.

"Actually," I bleated, "I'm fifty-five myself. But," I added hastily, "I can't believe that you're really that old." I appended a short, slightly hysterical laugh to this conciliatory ploy.

"I'm firefighter Pete," said the head, his grin widening so far that it looked as if it must circle his head and meet at the back of his skull. "And I'm twenty-seven, not fifty-five."

I shook my head in bewilderment. Some other planet must be missing these people, surely.

There was a pause during which no one spoke. I had reached a point of such concern about my physical welfare that I found it difficult to say anything.

"I think he's had enough of me," said the head. "I think I'll go away now. He's definitely had enough of me."

The head disappeared, and within seconds, so did the man who had been sitting next to me. I could hear them laughing together with their friends on the other side of the seat. I breathed a sigh of relief. Closing my eyes, I pretended to be asleep. In another twenty minutes we would be at my station, and that would be the end of that. Just a matter of sitting here and pretending that those men didn't exist.

And that would indeed have been the end of that, except that I overheard one more little snatch of conversation from the other side of the seat in front of me.

"It's that vicar bloke, innit? Off the telly."

"Oh yeah."

"You wanna get him prayin' for you. Get 'im to say a prayer for you. Go on!"

Pause.

"Naaah!"

I felt sick and angry with myself as I got off the train twenty minutes later and hurried off through the freezing night to find a taxi. I had done it again! Once more I had allowed myself to lose sight of the fact that the living, dynamic, involved Jesus was in that railway carriage, knowing those men in a way that no one else ever would or could. If I had kept my spiritual head, as it were, who knows what the power of God might have been able to do with that situation and those people, each of whom was and is, by some miraculous means, the most important person in the world. Oh, I don't kid myself. I doubt if they would have been spread-eagled round the floor of the carriage, zapped by the Spirit and surrendered to the Lord, but *something* might have happened if I hadn't so easily surrendered to the dreary logic and pressures of the world.

An act of the will is involved on these occasions, but my will had frozen and lost the power of action. May God forgive me and help me to do better next time. Actually, I am confident that he will do both of those things. He is a good Father. I really am beginning to think that he rather likes me.

LIMITLESS POSSIBILITIES

Something similar happened to the disciples on one famous occasion, of course, and it is recorded in the fourth chapter of Mark.

> On that day, when evening had come, he said to them, "Let us go across to the other side." And leaving the crowd behind, they took him with them in the boat, just as he was. Other boats were with him. A great windstorm arose, and the waves beat into the boat, so that the boat was already being swamped. But he was in the stern, asleep on the cushion; and they woke him up and said to him, "Teacher, do you not care that we are perishing?" He woke up and rebuked the wind, and said to the sea, "Peace! Be still!" Then the wind ceased, and there was a dead calm. He said to them, "Why are you afraid? Have you still no faith?" And they were filled with great awe and said to one another, "Who then is this, that even the wind and the sea obey him?" (4:35–41 NRSV)

Whatever the nature of the storm that is threatening, whether in a boat or on a train, it does seem a shame that we so easily lose our nerve and forget the inspiring things that have been done by Jesus in our lives in the past. We are so weak sometimes, aren't we? The encouraging aspect of all this, though, is that when we find fear and failure on one side of the coin, we are bound to find the limitless possibilities of our creative God on the other.

Let us pray for courage in the startlingly wide variety of situations that are bound to await us if we mean only half of what we say about following Jesus. We know that physical well-being cannot be guaranteed, and we can be sure that his idea of an ideal outcome may be very different from ours, but the only true place of safety in this universe is the centre of the will of God, as we already saw when we looked at the story of Jonah.

That police cell of mine was a bad enough place to end up in, but I can think of nothing more depressing than to spend the rest of my days locked in a small cell of fear and inaction, unable to leave, not because some heartlessly efficient outside police force is preventing me, but because the key is at the bottom of my own pocket, and I simply do not dare to take it out and use it.

Will we accept and face the risk that is automatically involved in following Jesus and putting him at the centre of our lives? Let us pray for courage.

My Encounters
with the Extreme Jesus

Tired, hot, and deeply annoyed with myself, I am sitting, slumped in a posture of defeat, at the bottom of a flight of stone steps. They lead up to the front door of a house in one of those endless suburban, terraced streets that seem to join and crisscross each other for mile upon indistinguishable mile across the north of London. I am very unclear about exactly where I am, and even less clear about how I will go about solving the problem that has arisen through my own foolishness. Beside me, on the pavement, stands my briefcase. Inside this black, spuriously efficient-looking container are the notes that I have made in preparation for a talk that I am almost certainly not going to be able to give about half an hour from now.

The fact is that I am lost. I am lost because I forgot to bring the details of my destination with me. Realising this omission when I arrived at Victoria Station, I decided not to phone home and check the details because I was sure I could remember which tube to get off at, and even the name of the church that was to be the venue for the evening. My confidence was completely misplaced. I alighted at the tube station that I thought was the right one, but after frantic enquiries and a lot of rushing around, I now know that I am in the wrong part of London. No one I have asked has ever heard of St Barnabas church, and when I rang home to check my information, nobody was there. The friend who is coming to pick me up has already left home and will discover that I am not where I should be and that his journey is a waste of time. I have no other numbers to ring.

Raising my eyes for a moment to cast a miserable glance around me, I see the silhouettes of four or five different churches, all at varying distances, their familiar but indistinct shapes rising like fairy-tale shadows above the eternal rows of terraced houses. One or two must be a great distance away. They seem to taunt me with seductive, unlikely possibilities.

"Perhaps it's me!" calls a ghostly grey spire that must be a good three or four miles away.

"No, no, I'm the one," booms a square, flag-poled tower in the next borough. "The people are all in here waiting for you. Come on, hurry up or you'll be late!"

But there is no point in tearing frantically around north London peering into random churches in the hope of hitting on the one that contains my abandoned congregation. Let's face it: this evening's event simply isn't going to happen, not with me there anyway. There is nothing left to do but to sit on this step. I have run out of ideas. I might as well be in the middle of a desert. I shall just stay here and cool down for a while, and then I shall go home. Oh dear. All those people will be sitting trustingly in rows, expecting me to turn up at any moment to talk to them. Tomorrow I suppose I will have to be brave and phone the organisers. Throw myself on their mercy. What a fool I've been! Whatever happened to the dynamic Christian living that you read about in books?

Suddenly I hear the sound of the front door opening and closing at the top of the steps behind me. I listlessly move aside to allow whoever it is to pass, but I do not bother to look up. There is a noise of feet hurrying down the steps, but then the footsteps stop. I look up. A man is standing there, head tilted, trying to get a better view of my face.

"Are you Adrian Plass?" he asks.

"That's right," I confess with the nervous little laugh I usually produce at these dignified moments.

"I've read your books," he says. "What are you doing up this way?"

"Well, not much," I tell him ruefully. "I'm in the wrong bit of London looking for a church called St Barnabas that doesn't exist."

"I know which part of London you should be in," he announces casually, "and I know exactly which church you're talking about. I saw something on a board about it the other night. I'm not going myself, but come and get in the car, and I'll take you there."

I am dumbfounded. He takes me there. It is the right place. I have arrived just in time. I thank my new friend for his help. He zooms off as I hurry into the church. The people who have come to this meeting turn out to be of the "three miracles before breakfast" persuasion and are obviously hoping that I am as well. Something nudges me to tell them the story of how I was stuck in the middle of nowhere and God sent a man out of the very house I was sitting in front of to make it possible for me to speak to them. I can talk the language when I need to. This goes down very well. Just up their street.

"But why don't you do it every time?" I ask God later.

He does not answer, but I suspect that my friend Ben, who collects me later from the meeting, gets close to the truth. He reckons that whenever possible without compromise, God does like to fit in with what's going on. Not only that, but he is more than happy to give people what they like as long as it's good for them, regardless of what some pessimists might say.

WHAT AM I SAYING?

I am standing at one of the counters in our local supermarket, waiting to pay for the goods that I have collected in my wire shopping basket. Two couples are ahead of me, so a few minutes will probably pass before it is my turn. I lay out my few objects carefully on the end of the mechanical rubber belt and then lean down to dump the empty basket on top of a little tower of identical ones on the floor. It is as I creak back to my full height once more and lift my head that my attention is drawn to the couple in front of me, or more precisely, to the female half of the couple in front of me. She is a dark-haired, sharp-featured woman in her fifties, well dressed, and with an air of relative prosperity. The voice that is emerging from her brightly painted lips is neither pleasant nor restful to the ear. She seems to have embarked on a lengthy voyage of complaint about every aspect of this shop, but something about the repetitive patterns in her speech suggests that she would search for and successfully discover something to get cross about in most situations.

"They really do seem incapable of organising themselves properly," she is saying to her husband in resonantly snappy schoolmarmish tones, "and we're the ones who have to wait around as a result, wondering how long it's going to take them to sort themselves out. Why they simply can't put more people on the checkout counters is beyond me. There seem to be enough of them hanging around up and down the aisles in the rest of the shop, doing nothing but gazing at shelves with their mouths hanging open like simpletons, trying to work out what's supposed to go in the gaps that should have been filled three hours ago by someone who's gone off for a fifteen-minute break that's lasted all morning. I blame the so-called managers. And I blame the people who employ them even more. Taking a boy out of school and training him for five and a half minutes before you put him in a bad suit and let him loose on what is supposed to be a commercial organisation serving the public, and what can you expect? Exactly the standard of service we're used to getting here – that is precisely what you can expect."

She looks at her husband for a response. He is a mild, rather nice-looking bald-headed man. He simply bows a little, like a reed that has learned the best way to deal with the prevailing wind, and says nothing. She looks at me and performs a little upward jerk of the head, presumably inviting me to agree with her vividly expressed sentiments. Seeing her face more clearly, and noting the negative lines etched into the skin around her eyes and her crimsoned mouth, I think how unhappy this woman looks. So angry and so unhappy. How should I respond to her? Normally, in a situation like this, I would probably smile in a noncommittal manner and make a noise that could be interpreted as agreement, disagreement, or a vague indication that given more time, I would have had things of great depth and insight to say on the subject.

Something is different this time though. Words are pushing to the front of my mind, and I have only a second or two in which to decide whether to let them out. Courage and cowardice, obedience and disobedience, these two coins get flipped so easily and so quickly in my fragile soul. I decide to say what I am thinking immediately, because any more than two seconds of reflection would result in my opting for the noncommittal smile. I just hope the origin of these words is what (or who) I think it is.

"You should look deep down inside the person you are," I say to her seriously, "find the softer part of yourself and bring it out so that you can show it to others."

This is not the kind of thing one normally says to complaining strangers in supermarket queues, and I wait with slight alarm to see how she reacts. Then there is her husband. He may have opted for the line of least resistance as far as his wife is concerned, but is there a chance that he will resent these words of gratuitous advice from a complete stranger and tell me to mind my own business? He simply smiles a whimsical little smile in the direction of his wife and bows his head again, as if lost in some familiar reflection.

His smile is not as broad as hers, though. I am amazed at the transformation. There are other creases in this woman's face. Perhaps they have not benefited from as much exercise as those lines of complaint and petulance that were so evident just now, but they are definitely there. She looks at me with real humour in her eyes.

"Perhaps I should," she says. "Yes, you're probably right. That's what I should do."

That is the end of our conversation, because the people right at the front of the queue have paid for their shopping and gone. Now the lady who complained so much and smiled with such unexpected warmth has moved forward with her husband to start packing their purchases into bags.

If I thought my comment was going to have a miraculously immediate, life-changing effect, I am doomed to disappointment. A few moments later, as they move away, she fiddling with something in her purse, he pushing their grocery bags in one of the supermarket trolleys, I can hear her expressing her equally negative views on the general management of their next destination, the drugstore on the other side of the pedestrian precinct.

Saying what I did just now was a waste of time and breath.

Was it?

Wasn't it?

Mind your own business.

All right.

Perhaps I am half a phrase in the fourth line of the fifty-ninth page of the long book of that lady's life. It is enough.

I find myself in one of those situations that are usually described by us evangelical Christians – rather gruesomely I have always thought – as "opportunities". I mean, of course, opportunities to witness to my faith. Quite straightforward, isn't it? I suppose it should be. Not for me, I'm afraid. At least not on this occasion. The person I am sitting with has started to talk about the different things that people believe.

"You're a Christian, aren't you?" he says, with genuine interest in his voice. "What's that all about, then?"

I feel my toes curling. I have written and spoken hundreds of thousands of words about what I believe and how I believe it and how everyone else ought to believe it but don't have to believe it if they don't want to, and goodness knows what else about every aspect of it, but now, suddenly, my tongue is tied. I think of that verse in the first book of Peter where the great apostle says that we should be ready to give a good account of our faith. I know we should. I should. But at this moment I can't. Why not? I don't know. It is as though I never was a Christian. I try to tell myself that my mission is to believers, not to unbelievers. I fail to persuade myself, because it is not true. Hastily I select a few harmless facts and minor feelings about my beliefs, tie them into a neat little package with a distracting bow on top, as it were, and hand it to him. He is clearly a little puzzled and not very impressed. It is hardly worth unwrapping. I don't blame him in the slightest. I would not be very impressed with what I have just said either. In my head the back of my mind screams angrily at the front.

"What! What is the matter with you? What is all that feeble bleating about? There is a passion in you for Jesus. You know there is. It makes you laugh and cry and do ridiculous things and go where you don't want to go. It gives you hope for the future and brings light into the darkness. It has turned you inside out, thrown you into the air, and caught you just before you hit the ground. Why don't you just spill some of that passion? Go on! Let it out! Tell him!"

But I can't. Sometimes I can. This time I can't. There seems to be nothing between the desert and the waterfall. My will is shrivelled. Some seedy human fear grips me, blocking the passage from my heart to my mouth. The person I was talking to leaves. I sit without moving for a long time. I look round once when I fancy I hear the sound of a cock crowing in the far distance. But it is just my imagination.

HARD TO CONCEIVE?

It is early evening, and I am travelling by taxi from Polegate, our nearest railway station, to Hailsham, the town where Bridget and I have lived for the last fifteen years. The driver of the cab is a pleasantly spoken, youngish man who has picked me up several times in the past. I recall the last occasion very well. He spoke to me about the disappointment he and his wife were experiencing because of her failure to conceive. Despite tests on both of them and treatment of every possible kind, there appeared to be little or no chance that they would be able to have a child, other than by adopting at some time in the future. I remember how much pain there was in him as he spoke of these things, and I also remember telling him that I would pray for a miracle for him and his wife. Doing such a thing is quite unusual for me. I seem to veer between not opening my mouth at all and opening it far too wide. Later that same evening I had, thank God, done exactly what I had promised. My life is littered with broken pledges relating to prayer, but this time I had stuck to my word.

"Any news on the baby front?" I ask foolishly and casually, fully prepared to hear him say that the situation has remained unchanged.

His face lights up.

"Yes! We're pregnant!" He realises what he has said and laughs. "I mean, my wife is pregnant. She's been—"

He breaks off, momentarily removing his attention from the road to look more carefully at my face. There is a note of puzzled conjecture in his voice as he continues haltingly.

"You're—you're the bloke who said you were going to pray for us, aren't you?"

I am indeed the bloke, but I don't know what to say. So much for all my teenage Christian dreams of actually being dramatically involved in one of those exciting testimony paperbacks that I used to read in the sixties.

Where's the script? Quick! Someone light the scene with powerful descriptive phrases. It's not quite the same in real life.

"Yes," I reply feebly, trying and miserably failing in my attempt to sound like a mighty prayer warrior who fully expects all his petitions to be answered comprehensively and promptly, "that's right."

He tells me more about his wife's pregnancy and how thrilled they both are about this unexpected turn of events. I tell him how very happy I am for them both. After a while we drive on in silence. So, I ask myself as we turn off the main road at the Arlington Eagles roundabout and head for Hailsham, is this an answer to my prayer or just a coincidence or a bit of both or what? And why am I asking these questions? What is the matter with me? Why can't I just connect the prayer to the outcome and leave it at that? Still, one thing's for sure. I'm ever so glad they're going to have a baby.

So am I.

And I really hope this might help both of them to find Jesus.

So do I.

I hope I don't get tempted in the future to tidy this all up, alter the timescale a bit, and offer it as evidence of my miracle-strewn close walk with God.

Oh, I hope that as well, even more than you do, believe me!

PAYING FOR THE DAMAGE

My wife, Bridget, and I are in Eastbourne, our nearest large town. We have come here to visit a shop, an establishment that always affects me in the same way. As we get out of the car after parking, I say to Bridget, "You know, there are two things I enjoy about this shop. One is arriving, and the other is leaving."

She nods in complete understanding. Blands Warehouse is basically a vast, unadorned barn of a place. It stocks an enormously wide range of products displayed in numberless towering canyons of shelving. You really can get just about anything here. Crockery, bedding, carpets, toys, beer, lighting, garden supplies, mirrors, bathroom fittings, luggage, large and small gnomes made out of painted plaster — the list is endless. The problem is that although prices are comparatively low, the actual quality of items on the shelves, certainly as far as elegance and style are concerned, can be depressingly poor. If you wish to buy, let us say, plain white plates, this is a good place to come. You will do well with things like that. Otherwise, Blands is a temple to bad taste. Bridget and I are well aware of this, but we never seem to learn. The phantom lure of economy draws us in, and then the blatantly awful standard of goods on offer causes us to flee in confusion.

There are exceptions to every rule. In the case of this shop, the exception is the furniture. Or rather one very specific line of furniture. A month or two ago, we discovered that Blands had begun to stock a new line of tables, chairs, dressing tables, and bookcases constructed from reclaimed timber. These pieces were attractive and interesting, incorporating as they did all the faults and imperfections of the old wood, planed and shaped to fit the new designs, but still pleasingly visible. The colour was good too. Waxed to a rich but subdued antique finish, the coffee table that we bought (for a truly inelegant and unstylish price) fitted perfectly with the other bits and pieces in our sitting room at home.

We are here today because we are thinking of purchasing another piece of furniture in the same line. Our old upright piano has died with one last despairing tinkle, and after the faded corpse has been removed, there will be a vacancy for something new against that part of the sitting-room wall. We know just what we want. There is a sideboard, first cousin to our coffee table, that we believe will be a perfect replacement for the departing piano. We are here today to look at it again and measure it and go through the ritual of those mutual reassurances and encouragements that inevitably precedes all of our major purchases.

On the way to the sideboard, we are distracted by a dressing table in the same line, a very nicely designed and constructed piece of furniture. It has a lovely gentle curve at the top of the mirror housing and a neat little drawer under each end of the work surface. The legs are really quite beautifully turned. A good price too. I decide to sit down so that I can get a better view of the underside of the dressing table. As I lower my weight onto what I have assumed is some variety of wooden chest, there is an ominous splintering sound from beneath me, and I make an abrupt descent for a distance of about three or four inches more than I had anticipated.

My response to this alarming event is a panic-stricken, struggling attempt to get up very quickly. This is ill advised. A further succession of cracks like pistol shots echoes around the vaulted roof of Blands Warehouse, and the descent of my person for another six inches or so renders any kind of swift ascent utterly impossible. I am now sitting right down inside the wooden chest with my legs dangling over one side. My wife gazes down at me in frozen disbelief. I am interested to know what she will say. Her comment, when it comes, seems to me a little lacking in compassion.

"It looks as if you've just bought yourself a smashed-up chest."

Watched by the small but fascinated audience of fellow shoppers that has gathered, I attempt to extricate myself from my wooden prison. At first my arms and legs flail helplessly, but nothing else moves. I have been in some undignified situations before, but this one takes the gold medal. Awful pictures form in my mind of my making a lurching, crouching, Quasimodo-like exit from the shop into the outside world wearing this box. Fuelled by the horrific pungency of this image, I engage in some more frantic struggling. After what seems an eternity, I am free and vertical again at last. It has taken about three violent goes. I notice that one or two members of my delighted audience are casting glances to the left and right, presumably wondering whether any of the shop staff have witnessed the destruction of one of their display pieces. They look mildly excited. I can understand that. Seeing others in conflict with authority when you haven't done anything wrong yourself has always been a prime spectator sport.

Perceiving that the clowning programme is over and that none of the Blands staff have witnessed my encounter with the chest, the audience drifts away, leaving Bridget and me to examine the damage I have caused. I sigh. It is extensive. There is no point in talking about repair. This box is a box no more. It is an ex-box, a pile of wood with some nails sticking out of it.

For one wild moment I contemplate the possibility of flight. I can remember avoiding responsibility for something similar once or twice in past years. If I were to walk straight out of the shop now, I could probably reach the safety of our car in time to make a clean getaway. The moment passes. Even if I were to seriously contemplate such a thing, I have to bear in mind that I am with Bridget. Between us we must surely have one whole conscience. No, there is no escaping it. We have just about internalised the fact that Christians don't break things and then run off, however much they may want to.

I set off to find a Blands employee and eventually discover a very young man sitting at a desk in the carpet department, deeply absorbed in the business of making a little pattern of holes in his blotter with a ballpoint pen.

"Excuse me," I say, "I wanted to tell someone that I've just destroyed a piece of your furniture by sitting on it."

The young man looks up from his blotter, suspending his activity in order to stare at me. A wild, hunted look appears in his eyes. His mouth opens and shuts silently. It is as though an alien has appeared and addressed him in the language of another planet.

"I'll show you," I suggest, realising that nothing is going to happen unless I say something else.

He nods dumbly, and I lead him down the shop to the scene of my accident. He looks at the thing that was once a chest and blinks heavily. Finally he mutters something about having to "fetch someone else" and hurries away down the nearest canyon where my wife is rather unconvincingly staring at horrible tea towels that she will never buy and pretending to be single.

Half a minute later another man arrives, presumably the young man's boss. This man is older, possibly in his mid-forties. He is quite smartly dressed and has a serious, troubled expression on his dark-complexioned face. Bridget gathers her courage together and comes over to linger near enough to hear what he has to say.

"Good afternoon," I say politely to the man. "I'm afraid I've broken one of your pieces of furniture by sitting on it. Look, it's this piece—I mean, these pieces—here."

He surveys the damaged box. He looks at me. He looks at Bridget. He looks at the box again. He looks around the shop. He rubs his chin with his hand. He looks at me once more. If his expression were a gearbox, it would be stuck in neutral. I do sympathise. I can see exactly what the problem is. Having sifted through the responses available to him after the years he has spent at Blands, he simply cannot find one that fits this situation. Should he adopt a stern, punitive approach in the face of this damage to property? Well, no, not really, because the damage was not deliberate, and the perpetrator has voluntarily confessed to his unpremeditated crime. Perhaps he should be lighthearted and matey. Well, no, not immediately, because he can't be sure yet if I am willing to pay for the damage. He ought to say something, but he can't. His lips begin to form words, but they never emerge from his mouth.

"I'll just fetch someone else," he manages at last, and he rides off down the same shelf canyon that swallowed up his young colleague a few minutes ago.

Bridget and I wait. As we hang around in the furniture department, we muse on the fact that we may have to work our way slowly up the entire Blands Warehouse command chain until we reach the chairman himself, who will drive down from some distant town with a couple of members of the board and make a final resolution possible. There is a short period during which nothing happens, and then the second man reappears. He has fetched someone else. He has brought a woman with him. She is quite different. She approaches the situation with authority and humour.

"If you don't like our furniture," she says with a twinkle in her eye, "why don't you just tell us instead of breaking it to pieces?"

We all laugh. The woman explains that the chest is not a chest at all. It is a fitment for the top of another, higher piece of bedroom furniture. That is why it was so flimsy. We ask her to tell us the price of the flimsy not-chest. She says it was just under a hundred pounds, but because of my honesty she will only charge us what it cost Blands to buy from the wholesaler. I express my thanks and conceal my horror. She asks the second man to go and find out how much that wholesale price is.

Bridget says to him, "Yes, and while you're gone, Adrian can sit down very carefully on one of these proper seats and jolly well think about what he's done!"

Up to this point the second man has continued to look uneasy. He smiles broadly at last on hearing me talked about as if I were a naughty child. He hurries away and returns a few minutes later to announce that the wholesale cost of the not-chest is fifty pounds. I find just enough money in my pocket and hand it over, trying to look and feel like a cheerful giver. I think I just about manage the look. He asks me if I would like to keep the piece of furniture that I sat on and in, and have now bought. When I say that I might as well, he picks it up, carries it to the customer service desk for me, and finds me a trolley so that I can transport it out to the car.

Just before we part he stops for a moment, looks very steadily into my eyes, and holds out his hand for me to shake. I could be wrong, but for him this seems to be a very important little piece of interaction. Perhaps in a small way he is encouraged to believe that there might be hope for humanity after all.

I feel a rush of relief as we drive away with our useless ruin of a box in the back of the car. I am relieved because I did resist the temptation to clear off and ignore my moral responsibility. Suppose this man, or any of the other people in the shop for that matter, had observed me making my craven escape and later seen my face on the cover of a book or learned in some other way that I claimed to be a follower of the one who never avoided a necessary confrontation in his life. A dreadful thought.

What a relief to know that Jesus shops at Blands Warehouse.

THE POWER AND THE GLORY

It is ten o'clock in the morning. I am sitting in my study at my computer working on this book. Bridget is out, taking my daughter to college because the rain is so heavy. I have fiddled about with some bits I wrote yesterday, changing the odd word here and there and looking for better ways to express what I wanted to say. Now I must get down to some solid work on a new section; otherwise my thousand words will never get written today.

Suddenly the hum of the computer dies away to silence and the screen goes blank. I become aware that all of the downstairs lights have gone out. The world, my world, seems to have stopped. It is what we call a power-cut. For some reason the electricity supply has ceased to function and a complete silence has fallen over the house. The first thing I think is that I might have lost all my "fiddles". As all writers will tell you, fiddles are not that easy to come by. I wonder if I shall be able to remember them when the power comes back on again.

But how long will it take? And is it only our house that has lost its electricity? I go along the hall and through the door into the garage to check the fuse box. No, all the little levers are pointing upwards, so the fuses are intact. I come back into the hall and open the front door. Standing in the doorway I find that the rain is still falling steadily from a charcoal-grey sky. Against this sombre background the leaves on nearby trees are a vivid, artificial green. One of those dark, oddly exciting mornings with the suggestion of a crackle in the air. I can see no lights in any of the surrounding houses, but most people are at work anyway, so that may not mean a great deal. Then, through the gaps in the bushes that separate us from the next house, I see our neighbour come out of her front door and look up at the sky. She is probably asking herself all the same questions as I am. I call through the gaps to her:

"Have you lost your electricity?"

"Yes," she calls back, "just a minute ago."

"Oh, good, it's not just me, then."

We wave and smile reassuringly at each other before retreating into our respective houses.

I am relieved. The fault is not one relating solely to our house. It is just a matter of waiting for the electricity company to put things right. I call Bridget on her mobile phone and ask her if we have plenty of candles in case the power-cut continues through to the evening. She assures me that we are well stocked with household candles.

That's that, then. What shall I do now? Make a cup of tea? I can't. The electric kettle won't work. I suppose I could boil the water in a saucepan on the gas ring. Yes, I might do that in a minute. I stroll into the sitting room and drop into my favourite armchair. The house seems oddly quiet without those vague humming noises that emanate from electrical appliances when they are working. I guess you tend not to notice those sounds until they are no longer available.

So what shall I do now? Can't carry on with the book for a bit. How can I usefully fill this space that has been unexpectedly presented to me? Has God given it to me for some reason? I cannot help smiling as I ask myself what my neighbour would say if I approached her with the appallingly egocentric hypothesis that she and most of the immediate neighbourhood have lost their electricity because God wants to create a space in my life. She might be rather cross. I doubt she has very much faith in the electricity company, let alone in God.

I decide to use some of this time to pray. I pray for my family one by one, for each of my three sons and their partners, for my daughter, Kate, for Bridget, and for myself. I rather enjoy praying into this profound silence. My fantasy is that God has turned everything off in order to be able to listen with even greater concentration than usual.

For a few moments after praying for myself, my mind is blank; then, with absolute clarity, a name floats out of the silence and hangs like a word on a placard at the front of my mind. It is the name of an old friend of mine, a Christian who has been involved in a number of working projects with me in the past. She is a capable, compassionate follower of Jesus, with a real desire to do the right things for God. I have not seen or heard from her for many months. Her name continues to hang there in front of me. It seems to glow as if it is illuminated by the love of God. What does that mean? Don't know. What shall I do about it?

I go to my study and look up her name in my address book. The address is there, but not the phone number. Perhaps this is all a bit silly. No, go on, find out the number and ring her. I contact directory enquiries and manage to get her number. When I ring the number, there is a pause before her husband answers and passes me on to her. I fear that I am not very coherent, but I do manage to convey the fact that her name came to my mind as I was praying and that God is lovingly with her in whatever she is doing or about to do. She tells me that she and her husband are in the process of making important life decisions and that there is much more she could tell me at another time and in another place. All in all, I am very glad that I phoned.

I go back to my armchair and sit in the empty silence once more.

"So," I say to God, "am I to believe that all this was organised just so that I would stay quiet long enough for you to say that name to me and get me to ring my friend?"

As usual God makes no audible reply, but at that moment the lights come back on. For a few seconds I do my expiring fish impression, and then I get up and go back to my study. The computer has recovered my "fiddles", thank God. Must get on. I have this book to write.

Some things can only be conjecture, but in my mind two things seem fairly sure. One is that the power is back, and the other is that it never went away.

EPILOGUE:
REVELATION

I wrote earlier about those warm souls with the hurt and peace in their eyes, and now I would like to introduce you to one of them, my grandfather, that is, my mother's father. Not that I ever actually met him. John Baker, a Sussex man and a farmer-turned-builder, died a few years before I was born. I have already mentioned his wife, Kitty Baker, who was my nana. She was the only person other than my mother in front of whom I was prepared to take off my clothes as a very small boy. Highly significant. She was found dead in bed one morning in the mid-fifties, on a day when she was supposed to be leading a bus party to London for a very early Billy Graham crusade. I was six at the time. She was the first major light to go out in my life. It was a terrible thing, my first encounter with the heavy grey twilight of bereavement. I mourned her death from the bottom of my small, darkened soul.

My mother was sustained throughout her life by the benefits of a very happy childhood. She loved both her parents and talked a lot about the father she had adored. Losing him at the end of the war was deeply painful. She told me often how kind and funny and reliable he was. Like his wife, he had been a devout Christian; he also was a part-time preacher at the little chapel in the country village where they lived.

Although I never met my grandfather, I had heard so much about him that he seemed to play a very real part in my life. As a child, I would gaze with deep fascination at his big framed photograph in the corner of the living room, wishing we could have met—just once. If only, I thought, he could have said a few words to me. He looked so nice. That was how I knew about the hurt and peace in his eyes. It was from looking at that old photo. I saw and appreciated it even as a child.

When I became a Christian, whatever that really means, at the age of sixteen, we sometimes sang a chorus that became very important to me. My life continued to be difficult and angst-ridden, despite my having said the statutory prayer of commitment and conversion. Nevertheless, somewhere in the centre of my storm-tossed teenage heart, an awareness had already taken root that with Jesus, potentially, anything was possible. I kept the words of this chorus in my heart, singing them silently to myself when everything else, including my new religion, was falling to pieces.

Turn your eyes upon Jesus,
Look full in his wonderful face;
And the things of earth will grow strangely dim
In the light of his glory and grace.

Writing about this brings back the feelings as well as the memories. What is the matter with me? My eyes are filling with tears as I write. Such a wretchedly failing Christian I was, if you judge as the world judges. Such a useless lad. Such dark misery and hopelessness. So hard on myself. How was I to know that in fact, I was as perfect a Christian as it is possible to be, a mess, a sinner saved by grace and loved by Jesus, just because I had sent out a feeble prayer like the thief on the cross, asking him to remember me now that he had come to his kingdom? How could I have received that extraordinary truth then?

Thousands of people find themselves in the same position. And please, if you are in the darkness now, take a moment to forget what you are and remember who and what he is. Be a sinner in his sight. Ask him to remember you, and he will say yes. Don't let them tell you that it works any other way. He knows how useless you and I are, and it is not a barrier, I promise.

Oh dear, got a bit carried away there, probably because of talking about my mother's family. Always an emotional area for me. But I meant it all. Every word.

So I must dry my eyes and continue with this little story. After I became a Christian, I was looking through some books in my mother's house when I happened to come across my grandfather's Bible. It was a traditional, old-fashioned, big black floppy volume, full of notes and comments added by its long-departed owner. I began to thumb through it, wishing as I had so often that he and I could have met and talked, especially now that we had Jesus in common. I had seen the Bible before, but I had never taken the time or trouble to look through it with any great care. I found it interesting now to read some of the observations and questions handwritten in the margins and to picture this man I had never seen in the flesh holding the book as I was holding it now while he studied or preached or listened to sermons.

I had flicked right through to the end of the Bible and was actually on the point of getting up from my chair to return it to the bookcase when I realised that my eye had been caught by something written on the inside back cover. I opened it up again and took another look. There it was. Inscribed in a much larger version of that beautiful copperplate handwriting were the words of the song that continued to sustain me when all else failed.

Turn your eyes upon Jesus,
Look full in his wonderful face;
And the things of earth will grow strangely dim
In the light of his glory and grace.

Perhaps those four lines had been as important to John Baker as they were to me. Certainly he had written them in large letters in a place that was easy to turn to at any time. I felt very touched by the thought that we had this small essential thing in common. I smiled at him across the years and thanked him for speaking to me at a time when it was so important and useful. He smiled back and said that it was a pleasure.

These little things that God does. So small. So vast. So sweet.

THE HOPE THAT BURNS WITHIN

My book is finished now, and the room at the other end of the hall has become a dining room again. Kathleen died in the middle of the afternoon on the twenty-third of February, just as the first hints of spring were beginning to appear in our garden. She has gone to be with Jesus. I suppose you cannot get much safer, more tender, and more extreme than that. By now the whole truth will have been revealed to her, and she will be amazed. Young, strong, bright-eyed, and filled with energy, she will take the Master's hand and hear him say to her, "Kathleen, I gave you five talents, and you have brought me ten. Well done, good and faithful servant! You have been faithful with a few things; I will put you in charge of many things. Come and share your Master's happiness."

We are very sad. We miss her. We love her. She loved us so much. She was and is a mark to aim for.

Do I have a 100 percent belief in her resurrection and eternal life? I have a 100 percent desire to have that much belief. I have a hope that burns inside me. It sometimes flickers. I have been promised that one day I shall go home to the Father's house. I guard that promise, but occasionally I forget where I have put it. I have a love for Jesus that has survived all the obstacles and pitfalls that have threatened to distract me from him since I was sixteen years old. I have in my heart the words of a song that continues to comfort me today as it comforted me then:

> *Turn your eyes upon Jesus,*
> *Look full in his wonderful face;*
> *And the things of earth will grow strangely dim*
> *In the light of his glory and grace.*

I think it's going to be all right.

PRAYERS
FOR THE
JOURNEY

SAFE JESUS

WHEN WE FEEL WEAK

Dear Jesus, you know how weak some of us are, how we come close to falling apart when something goes wrong, even though you have rescued us again and again in the past. You never condemn us for our fragility, and whenever possible you find a way to put us back on track so that we can reach the place where we will be useful to you.

We thank you for keeping a watchful eye on us, and especially when you order events so that our balance is restored and we can function adequately. We don't really mind feeling weak as long as you are there, Lord Jesus, but sometimes we get distracted and fail to even register the help you are offering.

It is so good to have you travelling with us. Help us to expect and be aware of your support. Amen.

WHEN WE ARE AFRAID

Heavenly Father, there are some dark and dreadful things in this world, and they feel even more frightening and oppressive when we simply do not understand them. We have learned from the Bible and from preachers and teachers that Jesus has defeated evil and that when we become his followers, we are safe from danger. The trouble is that it doesn't always feel like that.

When we are in the middle of what seems like a direct attack on our peace, it is so difficult to hang on to the freedom that is born in truth and to depend on the eternal safety that your Son bought for us on the cross. Thank you for his name, Father. Thank you for the name of Jesus. Thank you that when his name is whispered into the centre of the darkest whirlpool of fear, a change must occur. We need to believe this in our hearts as well as our minds, Father. Please help us. Amen.

WHEN WE FIND OURSELVES IN STRANGE SITUATIONS

Lord Jesus, it takes most of us many years to truly accept
that if we want to follow you, we must be content to find
our spiritual safety in a servant role. We know that we can
also be your friends if we obey you, but it is the obeying part
of the equation that is a bit tricky sometimes. The context
we find ourselves in will not always make us feel good about
ourselves, but it seems clear that you are able to reach and
touch people at the most unpromising times, and despite
our feelings of discomfort or failure.

Deepen our trust in you, Lord Jesus, so that we develop
a curious, confident fascination with what you might be
about to do, even in the most unlikely situations. We thank
you, Lord, for being willing to work through us. Give us the
courage and the humility to put your work before our sense
of well-being. Amen.

WHEN WE FEEL LIKE AN IDIOT

Lord Jesus, we all make idiots of ourselves at some point in our lives. And you do know how it feels. You were never an idiot, of course, but you did have to put up with people jeering at you and shaking their heads and wagging their fingers when you ended up on the cross and they thought you had failed. I am so sorry that you had to go through that, enduring such scorn from the very people you had come to save.

I seem to make an idiot of myself on a fairly regular basis, but I am afraid there is no secretly interesting and virtuous basis for it. I'm just an idiot sometimes. Thank you for keeping me safely in your family and putting up with me and smiling at me and encouraging me to keep going and finding opportunities for me to work for you, knowing full well that I am likely to make a whole set of completely new mistakes.

The thing I think we would all like to ask you for is this: when the right time comes for us to present ourselves to the world as idiots or fools for you, we want to have the kind of faith and courage that enabled your old servant Noah to build a huge ship where there was no water. They laughed at him. Of course they did. I expect they will laugh at us. Be with us when that happens, Father. We would hate to fail you. Amen.

WHEN WE DOUBT

Lord Jesus, because we are all different, each of us deals with doubt at different times and in different ways, but not one of us welcomes the problem. It makes us feel that we are betraying you, and it can undermine the peace and the security that are part of our relationship with you when things are at their best.

We thank you that you have given us the gift of faith, and we ask you to remind us that because of this gift, belief in you is our natural state. Guide us towards good habits in our thinking, and forgive us when we knowingly embrace ideas or experiences that lead us away from the place where we have confidence in you.

Thank you for your gentleness in dealing with us over these matters, and may we be as gentle with others when they meet the same obstacles. Amen.

FOR OUR FAMILY MEMBERS IN THE CHURCH

Father, it must give you great pleasure to see how your church looks after itself when things are going right. We feel a rush of gratitude when we think of the fact that we have brothers and sisters all over the world, a family whose members look to you for guidance in their dealings with the world and with each other. Father, when we look back we can see how you have led people into our lives when we needed them. Help us not to let you and each other down when there is something we can do. Ours is not a perfect family, but it is a lovely one, and you delight in it. Thank you for being our Father. Amen.

FOR RESPECT AND UNITY IN THE CHURCH

Lord Jesus, there is a deep and thrilling mystery at the heart of the idea that the church really is your body here on earth. I find it fascinating and reassuring to think that those who genuinely follow you are connected, not just by words or a set of ideas, or even by sharing the same faith, but by a supernatural bond that is ultimately more real and indissoluble than any mere physical chain.

Teach us to absorb and accept this fact, Lord, and as a consequence to offer the same kind of respect and service to our brothers and sisters as we would offer to you. This is not easy, Lord Jesus. The temptation to judge others is always with us, and we give in all too easily. Let your heart be in our hearts, and your mind in our minds, so that we can feel as you feel and think as you think, and may the unity of the Holy Spirit keep us safe by binding us to each other and to you forever. Amen.

FOR OUR SAFETY IN JESUS

What a joy it is to feel safe in you, Lord Jesus. Not entirely safe yet, but travelling in that direction. I go hot and cold when I think about times in the past when I must have trampled all over things that other people were trying to say to me, things that were important to them and needed to be heard. I suppose a lot of it was to do with the fact that I was trying to convince myself just as much or even more than the person I was talking to. I didn't feel very safe in those days, did I?

Lord, do you remember that lady I met in Liverpool? Well, of course you do. You don't have memory problems like we do. She told me that she felt she had met you for the first time in her sessions with properly trained Christian counsellors. When I asked her exactly what she meant, she explained that it was the first time she had been listened to without being interrupted with advice or warnings or Bible verses or suggestions for prayer. They listened to her, Lord Jesus, and in their patient listening she met you.

Thank you for letting us be in the place where you live, Lord. Now we can run errands for you and remain calm and confident because we know our way home. Amen.

TENDER JESUS

WHEN WE FEEL SORRY FOR OURSELVES

Lord Jesus, sometimes we are so lost in the swamp of our own failure and inadequacy that we forget how your heart is continually broken by the conflict and selfishness of this fallen world. Forgive us for surrendering to self-pity, and give us a new determination to join you in making a difference in the way things are. On our own we may not be able to do much, but with your guidance and wisdom, the little that we do might be more significant than we shall ever know until we meet you face-to-face.

Oh Lord Jesus, you know how defeated we feel sometimes. Lift us and refresh us. Warm our hearts with your own tenderness, and energise us for the next thing that has to be done. Amen.

WHEN WE HAVE DONE WRONG

Lord Jesus, some situations simply go beyond words.
Sometimes resentment and fear result in our disobedience,
and there is nothing left but to throw ourselves on your
mercy as a child throws him- or herself on the mercy of a
wise, loving parent.

In these times you know that I like to pray the wonderful
Prayer of Humble Access, a part of the Anglican Communion
service that is repeated by the minister and congregation
shortly before bread and wine are distributed.

We do not presume to come to this thy table, O merciful Lord,
trusting in our own righteousness, but in thy manifold and great
mercies. We are not worthy so much as to gather up the crumbs under thy table. But thou art the same Lord, whose property is always
to have mercy . . .

Yes, you are the same tender Lord. Whatever the nature
of the sins we may be confessing, if we truly repent, you will
have mercy yet again and take us by the hand and lift us
up and assure us that nothing has changed. There will be a
smile and a new beginning and a new chance and a shout of
joy in heaven because that awkward sheep is back in the fold
again. Thank you. Amen.

WHEN WE NEEDLESSLY REOPEN OLD WOUNDS

Father, sometimes it can be quite a surprise to suddenly realise how much you have done in our lives and how far you have brought us since we first met you. I wonder how many of us are still feeling pain from wounds that were actually healed a long time ago. Quite a lot, I should imagine. Does it hurt you, Father, to find that we, your children, are still hanging on to a negative past that has no power to injure anymore, and that we have somehow failed to focus on the changes that have made that possible?

Forgive us, Father. We just don't seem to see the most obvious things sometimes. Open our eyes to the work you have done in and for us. Give us thankful hearts. We are grateful for your gentle healing touch. Please don't be sad. Amen.

WHEN WE NEED TO SEE YOU CLEARLY

Dear Lord Jesus, C. S. Lewis really did get it about right with Aslan, didn't he? I'm talking about the fact that the children in those stories didn't actually see the great lion on very many occasions. They would encounter all sorts of difficulties and dilemmas and get quite troubled about the possible outcome of their problems, but Aslan, famously not a "tame" lion, only appeared at those crucial moments when a clear sight of him was what the situation demanded.

In our lives, Lord, you allow us these moments when we see glimpses of your face. Help us to keep our eyes open for the sudden vision of you sitting next to us or waving from the corner of the room or standing on the far horizon. These visions of your tender love make all the difference when the going gets tough, and we do not want to miss them. Amen.

FOR THOSE WHO CARE FOR OTHERS

We thank you, Lord Jesus, that there are people in the church who have taken you seriously. They are intent on the business of reflecting your tenderness, and their service to others is often a sacrificial one. Why is it, Lord, that folk like this are so convinced that they have little to offer as your followers? One thing is for sure. It makes them even more attractive as people. We should nurture them and give thanks for them and try to learn a lesson from them.

All over this country and all over the world, I am blessed by continually meeting Christians who put all their energies into caring more for others than for themselves. Sometimes this involves physical danger, and sometimes sheer hard work. We do not ask peace for them as the world gives peace, Lord Jesus, but we do ask you to guard the most important part of them and to give them strength to continue.

Bring them at the end to your heavenly garden and let them smell the roses and rejoice. May we all aspire to reflect your love, and may we never believe that we have succeeded. Amen.

WHEN A LOVED ONE IS DYING

Lord Jesus, some of the people who are reading this book
will be dealing with bereavement or with the prospect of
losing a person they love. It's all very well for me to wrap
up the whole thing in words, but I know it's not like that
really. It's not neat. It's not tidy. There are moments when
everything seems to fall apart and all you want to do is cry
or scream or get really angry with someone. Sometimes faith
disappears altogether and life seems pointless.

Lord, I know that you understand all those feelings and
failures. I know that you weep with us and long for the time
when we will be able to see that all things really are well.
Thank you for those who have loved us, the ones who are
still with us and the ones we have lost. And thank you so
much for your courage in the face of death and separation
from your Father. Because of that courage we are secure in
the knowledge that we shall be able to see our loved ones,
such as my mother-in-law, Kathleen, again. Amen.

WHEN SOMEONE WE KNOW IS BEREAVED

Lord Jesus, some of us talk an awful lot of rubbish about strength in bereavement. I've done it myself and felt ashamed. In doing so we have sometimes been guilty of adding needless guilt to the burden of those who are already experiencing deep and crippling pain.

We want to thank you for simply being in the middle of it with us, for legitimising our pain through making it your own. Sometimes there are no answers, and we ask you to protect us from the temptation to invent them for others purely because we are unable to deal with the way we are feeling ourselves.

One day we shall understand what all these things mean, but in the meantime we put our trust in you. You know what it means to suffer as a human being, and we thank you for shedding tears with us in all our troubles.

We pray especially for your blessing on those who feel that they have lost you as well as the one they loved. That is a dark tunnel indeed. May we be willing to enter it with those who suffer, and simply stay quietly there beside them until they feel able to raise their eyes and once more consider the possibility of light. Amen.

EXTREME JESUS

WHEN WE NEED COURAGE

Lord Jesus, we have no idea where you will take us if we make the decision to follow you, but we really don't want to let you down when the crunch comes. Whether we are falling through the holes in our lives or facing disturbing situations or simply trying to represent you to those whom we meet every day, help us to turn our eyes away from the security of this world and focus on you. We know that there will be risks and challenges and even danger in the places to which you lead us. Prepare us, support us, give us courage, forgive us when we stumble and lose heart.

Thank you, Lord Jesus, for dying for us. Thank you for persevering with us. Thank you for tilting the world on its axis. Stay close, Lord. Amen.

WHEN WE FAIL TO ACT

Jesus, we call you Lord, but there are times when we let you down very badly and feel embarrassed by our own presumption in claiming to follow you. Why does it happen? Why do we dry up sometimes when the need, the task, is clearly there before us? Why do we do that? We don't want to be that person, Lord. We don't want to be that cowardly person who retreats when going forward might change a life or bring hope into a situation. We want to follow you to the edge.

Thank you for forgiving us and encouraging us when we fail to do so. Help us to practice being in your presence so that we are always conscious of your being there when we are with others. Strengthen us, Lord. Thank you. Amen.

WHEN WE ARE WITH ANNOYING PEOPLE

Yes, I know, I know, of course I know that there are no
unimportant people in the world, but, Lord, do we really
have to spend time with people who just get on our nerves?
I'm sure I can't be a very good or useful person to talk to
a certain someone. I start breathing heavily through my
nose and blinking with exasperation within a few seconds
of being with her. I do try to react differently, but that's the
effect she has on me.

Yes, all right, don't worry, I know exactly what you want
to say to me about this. Do I realise how many people have
been patient with me in the past when they would much
rather have been doing something else? Do I honestly
believe that following you gives me the freedom to pick and
choose who I am going to spend time with?

I do accept the answers to those questions, and I do
want to be obedient. It's just hard, Lord, really hard. I don't
approve of myself over this issue. Neither do you. Take my
hand and help me. Thank you. Amen.

WHEN WE SPEAK TO OTHERS

Sometimes, Lord Jesus, we have only seconds in which to make a decision about saying or doing something that may have an effect on another person's life. We hesitate for obvious reasons. We might be completely wrong in thinking that the impetus comes from you. That can easily happen. Then there is the very human fear of attracting a response that might be hostile or scornful.

We can only ask, Lord, that you will help us to be wise and brave, wise enough to weigh the impulse quickly and brave enough to say the words with confidence if we still feel that they are the right ones.

For many of us this a new way of being in the world, yet it is the way that you walked, for you only did what you saw the Father doing. It scares us, Lord. Stay close. Amen.

WHEN WE NEED TO TAME OUR TONGUE

Father, those of us who sometimes have difficulty keeping our mouths shut may need to be reminded of these words from the book of James:

When we put bits into the mouths of horses to make them obey us, we can turn the whole animal. Or take ships as an example. Although they are so large and are driven by strong winds, they are steered by a very small rudder wherever the pilot wants to go. Likewise the tongue is a small part of the body, but it makes great boasts. Consider what a great forest is set on fire by a small spark. The tongue also is a fire, a world of evil among the parts of the body. It corrupts the whole person, sets the whole course of his life on fire, and is itself set on fire by hell.

All kinds of animals, birds, reptiles and creatures of the sea are being tamed and have been tamed by man, but no man can tame the tongue. It is a restless evil, full of deadly poison. (3:3–8)

Heavenly Father, this "restless tongue" syndrome really is one of the great challenges to members of the Body of Christ. There is an appetite for gossip and criticism in most of us, and indulging that appetite can be very enjoyable. But in the final analysis it is an empty, loveless enjoyment, and we do not assent to this tendency in us.

Strengthen us, Father, in our resolve to tame our tongues by an effort of the will, holding back, even when they are true, those words that might directly or indirectly damage another person without bringing benefit to anyone. May we be equally ready to open our mouths fearlessly or generously at the right time, according to your will. Thank you. Amen.

FOR AN UPSIDE-DOWN VIEW OF THE WORLD

Lord Jesus, sometimes we need a lesson in perspective and focus, of the topsy-turvy way in which you view the world, the first coming last and the last first. It frightens us to see how easily we can move away from that understanding and begin to measure the worth of people and activities according to the way of the world.

Give us an eye test, Lord, all those of us who need it. Remind us that you see things, and especially people, in your own very compassionate and creative way. Sharpen our focus, Lord, so that we don't waste time and energy on irrelevancies. Amen.

WHEN WE PONDER YOUR MYSTERIOUS WAYS

Father, I really don't understand you sometimes. That probably does not come as a great surprise to you. I have difficulty in comprehending bus timetables, let alone the Creator of the universe. Actually, thinking about it, that's not a very good example. Bus timetables are virtually impenetrable. But you know what I mean.

Sometimes I wish I could see behind the scenes, as it were. How does it all operate, Father? How is it all arranged? And why does it seem to go like clockwork on some occasions and not at all on others?

We can never actually predict what you are going to do in any given situation, can we? I'm glad it's you in charge and not me. Thank you for looking after us, Father, for making all the plans and carrying them out. Thank you. Amen.

WHEN WE WITNESS A MIRACLE

Lord Jesus, a lot is said about signs and wonders and
miracles, but when one might have actually happened, we
seem to be so amazed that we can hardly accept it. Perhaps
our expectations are too low. Perhaps we should be more
open and more optimistic about such things. It is much
wider than that, though, isn't it? We should be prepared for
absolutely anything to happen in a situation where you are
present and involved.

May the Holy Spirit wake us up to the endless
possibilities of a life that is centred on you, and when the
time is right, help us to be bold in talking about your love
and power to those who do not know you. You want to
change the world, Lord, and we want to help you. Amen.

FOR STRENGTH FOR THE ADVENTURE

How strangely you work in our lives. We can never predict what you will do next. We're glad. It would be much less of an adventure if we were able to know exactly what was going to happen when we got up on a Monday morning.

Lord, you won't leave us alone. And we don't want you to. We don't want you to ever leave us alone. We want the adventure to carry on, right up to the extreme edge of your will for us. Mind you, we may pray this now in the middle of a burst of enthusiasm. Tomorrow we might lose our nerve. We hope not.

Breathe your strength into us, Lord, so that we will not lose heart when the next order comes. Amen.

MY PRAYER FOR YOU

Lord Jesus, I pray for the person you love and who is reading these words at this moment. Bring them home, Lord. Whatever else happens, bring them home. Amen.

The Sacred Diary of Adrian Plass, on Tour
Aged Far Too Much to Be Put on the Front Cover of a Book
Adrian Plass

We got our first taste of Adrian Plass's outrageous humour in *The Sacred Diary of Adrian Plass Aged 37 3/4* and *The Sacred Diary of Adrian Plass, Christian Speaker, Aged 45 3/4*. With over 2 million copies sold, these beloved bestsellers naturally placed the author's fanciful alter-ego in great demand as an inspirational speaker. And of course, his touring experiences have led to all-new stories to share with his friends. This sequel to the first two books will doubtless secure the Sacred Diarist's reputation as a spiritual authority. It's probably not the reputation he's hoping for, but it's the perfect medium for a bucketful of laughter. So meet the speaker, meet the crew and take a seat. It's time to join Adrian Plass on tour!

> *Anne seems to think it would be a good idea to let people see some of the diary entries I've written in connection with the little seven-day speaking tour that she and I have just done...*

On that innocent note, Adrian Plass whisks us along on one of the zaniest tours in his career as a Christian speaker. Besides his wife, his fictional entourage includes Gerald, his grown son, who is now a wisecracking vicar; high-strung Leonard Thynn and his talented but surrealistic girlfriend, Angels Twitten; and the tour's Scripture-spouting benefactor, Barry Ingstone. First stop is the church of St. James the Hardly Visible at All, where a dour caretaker is waiting to set the tone for things to come. So hop on board – the tour is leaving, and you don't want to miss a thing.

Jacketed Hardcover: 0007130457

Pick up a copy today at your favourite bookstore!

GRAND RAPIDS, MICHIGAN 49530 USA

WWW.ZONDERVAN.COM

The Sacred Diary of Adrian Plass Aged 37 3/4

Adrian Plass

A laugh-filled, fictional daily chronicle of family and church exploits, featuring Adrian Plass's literary alter ego and a memorable cast of supporting characters.

> *Saturday, December 14th*
> *Feel led to keep a diary. A sort of spiritual log for the benefit of others in the future. Each new divine insight and experience will shine like a beacon in the darkness!*
> *Can't think of anything to put in today.*
> *Still, tomorrow's Sunday. Must be something on a Sunday, surely?*

Adrian Plass is hilarious, pure and simple. His readers are legion – and this is the bestselling book that started it all, converting thousands of people who love to laugh into avid Plass readers.

The Sacred Diary of Adrian Plass Aged 37 3/4 is merriment and facetiousness at its best – a journal of the wacky Christian life of Plass's fictional alter-ego, who chronicles in his 'sacred' diary the daily goings-on in the lives of ordinary-but-somewhat-eccentric people he knows and meets. Reading it will doeth good like a medicine!

Softcover: 0310269121

Pick up a copy today at your favourite bookstore!

ZONDERVAN™

GRAND RAPIDS, MICHIGAN 49530 USA

WWW.ZONDERVAN.COM

The Sacred Diary of Adrian Plass, Christian Speaker, Aged 45 3/4

Adrian Plass

Adrian Plass lovers got their initial baptism of laughter through his bestseller, *The Sacred Diary of Adrian Plass Aged 37 3/4*. The author's account of 'serious spiritual experiences' naturally made him in demand as a public speaker – so of course another diary was inevitable.

The Sacred Diary of Adrian Plass, Christian Speaker, Aged 45 3/4 continues the misadventures of Adrian's fictional alter-ego. As Plass gathers regularly with his support group, we meet old friends, including his longsuffering wife, Anne; son Gerald, now grown but no less irrepressible; loony and loveable Leonard Thynn; Edwin, the wise church elder; and Richard and Doreen Cook, who are just as religious as ever. We also meet some new characters, such as Stephanie Widgeon, who only seems to have one thing to say, ever . . . and who knows, we might even find out why Leonard Thynn borrowed Adrian's cat all those years ago.

And finally – what is a banner ripping seminar?

Softcover: 031026913X

Pick up a copy today at your favourite bookstore!

GRAND RAPIDS, MICHIGAN 49530 USA

WWW.ZONDERVAN.COM

From Growing Up Pains to the Sacred Diary
Nothing Is Wasted

Adrian Plass

Two favourite works by bestselling author Adrian Plass in one volume

Adrian Plass has a way of telling our stories by telling his, and by so doing has endeared himself to a multitude of readers. Perhaps his secret lies in his humour, from the dark to the absurd. Or it could be his penchant for poking gently but frankly at the foibles of Christian living. Both qualities are on display here, with two of Plass's best-loved books rolled into one.

The Growing Up Pains of Adrian Plass offers reflections on a difficult passage in the author's personal journey, during which the television programme *Company* and some of its memorable guests made a deep impact on Plass's faith. *The Sacred Diary of Adrian Plass Aged 37 3/4* is a laugh-filled, fictional daily chronicle of family and church exploits, featuring Plass's literary alter ego and a memorable cast of supporting characters.

Referring to *The Sacred Diary*, Plass writes, 'I don't think I shall ever be unhappy enough to write such a funny book again.' Though different in character, both books in this volume explore the darker side of living the Christian faith – and, in Plass's inimitable style, point beyond to the bright hope that lies in Jesus

Softcover: 0310278570

Pick up a copy today at your favourite bookstore!

ZONDERVAN™

GRAND RAPIDS, MICHIGAN 49530 USA

WWW.ZONDERVAN.COM

The Sacred Diaries of Adrian, Andromeda and Leonard

Adrian Plass

Three bestselling books – three times the laughter – all in one delightful collection of vintage Adrian Plass.

Bestselling author Adrian Plass takes us on a rollicking tour of his slightly surreal world. From the pungent Andromeda Veal to the loony, loveable Leonard Thynn to Plass's longsuffering wife and irrepressible son, the 'Sacred Diarist' and company are here in full glory, bound for misadventure, loads of fun, and the occasional insight neatly camouflaged as humour.

The Sacred Diary of Adrian Plass, Christian Speaker, Aged 45 3/4 – After his account of 'serious spiritual experiences' in *The Sacred Diary of Adrian Plass Aged 37 3/4*, Plass is in demand as a public speaker – and of course, that calls for a brand-new diary!

The Horizontal Epistles of Andromeda Veal – Budding young Christian feminist Andromeda Veal has broken her femur and now lies in traction. But she's still entirely capable of responding in her own inimitable style to the letters she receives from Adrian's wife and fellow churchgoers.

The Theatrical Tapes of Leonard Thynn – If suffering produces character, chairing the church play ought to produce integrity by the truckload for Plass as he contends with the likes of Percy Brain, Victoria Flushpool, Vernon Rawlings and other unforgettables.

Softcover: 0310278589

Pick up a copy today at your favourite bookstore!

ZONDERVAN™

GRAND RAPIDS, MICHIGAN 49530 USA

WWW.ZONDERVAN.COM

Nothing But the Truth
A Collection of Short Stories and Parables

Adrian Plass

A parable can 'entertain at the front door while the truth slips in through a side window,' and few Christian writers can tell one as deftly as Adrian Plass. In this collection of short stories he is thought-provoking, inventive and easily able to traverse that short distance between a smile and a tear.

Combining material from *Father to the Man* and *The Final Boundary* and introducing a fresh new story, *"Nothing But the Truth"* reveals the more serious side of Adrian Plass. Seasoned with his trademark humour, the stories portray characters responding to emotional or spiritual crises – and in so doing, reveal truths about ourselves, the games we sometimes play and the love we all are searching for.

Softcover: 0310278597

Pick up a copy today at your favourite bookstore!

ZONDERVAN™

GRAND RAPIDS, MICHIGAN 49530 USA

WWW.ZONDERVAN.COM